The Best
Ice Cream Maker
Cookbook Ever

The Best
Ice Cream Maker
Cookbook Ever

Peggy Fallon

A John Boswell Associates/King Hill Productions Book
HarperCollins*Publishers*

HarperCollins books may be purchased for educational, business, or sales promotional use. For inform-ation, please e-mail the Special Markets Department at SPsales@harpercollins.com.

Design: by Barbara Aronica
Index: Maro Riofrancos

ISBN 0-06-018765-4

16 17 18 RRD 28 27 26 25 24 23

Acknowledgments

Thanks again to Susan Wyler, my editor, who makes good things even better.

And to JMG, who endured many a frosty evening while ice cream machines whirred in the kitchen. He also came to the rescue when my computer printer gasped its last breath in the middle of Chapter Five.

Contents

CHAPTER ONE. MAKE MINE ICE CREAM   9

Pick any one of the 36 great flavors featured here, and you're sure to be delighted. From the best of the basics—French Vanilla, Classic Chocolate, Sensational Strawberry, Butter Pecan—to tantalizing new flavors like Espresso Bean, Raspberries 'n' Cream, Double Ginger, and Lemon Custard.

CHAPTER TWO. SWIRLS AND TWIRLS   53

Add-ins, dollop-ons, and toppings include ice creams—Mint Chocolate Chip, Eggnog Cranberry Swirl, Praline Swirl, Chunky Peanut Fudge Ripple—sauces— Hot Fudge, Best Butterscotch, Easy Caramel—and garnishes such as Chocolate Curls and Twirls.

Introduction

The Whole Scoop

When I told an acquaintance the subject of this cookbook, his immediate response was, "So it's a book on making desserts?" I must admit I was a bit perplexed for a moment, as I have always thought of ice cream in a class by itself. Ice cream is more than a dessert, it's . . . well . . . a treat, a sensory experience.

Ice cream is cool comfort for adults and the stuff children's dreams are made of. It's that icy gratification stolen on a Saturday afternoon, that welcome pick-me-up on a stifling hot day—and sometimes on a cold rainy one—the traditional finale to the annual spaghetti-feed at the church hall. It even makes a tonsillectomy worthwhile. Ice cream is what you eat when you fall in love or when you have a broken heart. Ice cream is something that is given as a reward and withheld as punishment.

Ice cream can be devoured directly from its carton while you're standing in front of the freezer or when you're hiding under the bedcovers. It can be licked from a cone as you drive along a country road or spooned graciously from frosty silver coupes at an elegant restaurant.

I'm here to report to all former kids that at least one thing in life has gotten easier. After trying them all, I can say with some authority that machines designed for home ice cream making can now be ranked from "easy" to "easiest." The labor required is minimal and the results are utterly fantastic. Along with this mechanical renaissance comes a myriad of applications for your ice cream machine.

Ice cream now seems to be a generic term for just about any frozen sweet. Though we like to claim it as American, it is really an international favorite. Italians introduced us to the pure and vibrant flavors of their *gelato,* a dense yet soft ice cream rich with egg yolks but generally lower in butterfat than traditional American flavors. In addition to the classic French custard-based *glacée,* which is similar to commercially made premium ice creams, and Philadelphia-style ice cream, made with no eggs, there are "ice creams" that contain no cream at all. Premium frozen yogurts, low-fat ice creams, sorbets, and icy granitas have all gained tremendous popularity in our health-conscious era. And the best news is that whether rich and creamy or lean and icy, all are now a breeze to make at home.

Meet Your Maker

To ensure you enjoy making ice cream whenever you feel like it, it's important to choose the style of maker that's right for you. In the beginning, there was the large wooden hand-cranked ice cream freezer, and they're still thriving today. In deference to modern times they've now added an electric version, but the principles remain the same. A chilled ice cream base is poured into the heavy stainless steel ice cream canister, fitted with a sturdy stationary paddle called a dasher. The canister is covered and placed inside the wooden bucket, connected to a support arm, and continuously rotated by either hand-cranking or electric power.

Freezing is accomplished by surrounding the canister with layers of crushed or shaved ice and coarse rock salt, a mix that melts to create an icy brine that lowers the temperature of the churning ice cream until it reaches its freezing point. The gradually melting ice usually freezes the mixture in 25 to 35 minutes. Rapid freezing in this manner causes many small ice crystals to form, which ultimately produces a smooth-textured ice cream. Aerating these crystals by rotating the dasher, or paddle, prevents ice chunks or flakes from forming. These nearly indestructible 4-quart and 6-quart machines are valued for more than nostalgia; they make excellent ice creams, sorbets, and frozen yogurts. These models are a bit pricey, but they're a lifetime investment for those who want to make large batches of ice cream.

Other American manufacturers have taken the electric salt-and-ice bucket freezer idea a little further, creating a sturdy plastic machine with a metal canister and a maximum capacity of 2 quarts. The appeal of this model is that it doesn't require any special supplies; it freezes the mixture in 20 to 30 minutes by layering 4 standard trays of ice cubes from your freezer with ordinary table salt and cold water. The texture of the finished product depends largely on how fast it is processed.

Because ice cubes melt slowly and table salt dissolves quickly, the icy brine needed for smooth ice cream is created less quickly than in the previously mentioned, more traditional models. Slowly adding ½ to ¾ of a standard (26-ounce) box of table salt to the ice according to the manufacturer's directions will ultimately produce a silky ice cream. I've used one of these reasonably priced models for at least 10 years, and I'm always pleased with the finished product.

About 10 years ago, a handy, affordable freezer took ice cream lovers by storm and is probably responsible for today's widespread enthusiasm for making ice cream at home. In this simple "machine," sometimes called a Donvier-type freezer after the Japanese company that invented it, a prechilled canister eliminates the need for ice and salt. This type of ice cream maker comes in half-pint, pint, and quart sizes and features a sealed, hollow metal canister that is filled with a special space-age coolant. This canister must be frozen for at least 24 hours before it is used. To make sure it is at proper temperature, shake the canister when you remove it from the freezer. If you hear any liquid sloshing around inside, turn down the setting on your freezer to make it colder, return the canister to the freezer, and try again later.

The frozen canister is filled with the ice cream base and fitted inside a simply designed plastic bucket—no ice, no salt, no electricity. Just cover the cylinder, attach the handle, and turn it twice every 3 minutes. The ice cream forms on the cold walls of the frozen container. When you turn the handle, it scrapes the ice cream off the walls and into the warmer center of the mixture. Like magic, after about 20 minutes you have ice cream, sorbet, or frozen yogurt. There are only minor problems with this design. The canister takes up a considerable amount of freezer space, and because little air is incorporated during the churning process, the finished ice creams become quite hard when stored in the freezer. Also, the canister must be again frozen for 24 hours before making another batch. Nonetheless, for small batches of ice cream that are to be eaten the same day, this model is a great value.

Several appliance makers have created an electric machine built to house a 1- to 1½-quart prechilled canister. You still face the problem of storing the double-insulated canister in the freezer a minimum of 6 to 22 hours for each batch, but once that's done, it's a breeze. The frozen canister is immediately placed on the motor base, fitted with the plastic dasher, covered with a clear plastic top, and turned on. There is a generous opening in the plastic cover, through which you pour in the ice cream base. (You can also use it later for add-ins.) The see-through lid lets you watch your ice cream being made; it usually takes 20 to 30 minutes.

This method seems to incorporate more air into the mixture, for I didn't experience the same storage problems as I did with the manual Donvier. Although I felt a certain amount of loyalty to my somewhat messy old ice-and-salt machine, this one is so simply designed and easy to use I have created permanent space in my freezer to store the canister.

I also bought a less expensive version of this type of machine, where a small motor is fitted on top of the frozen canister. The opening on the see-through plastic lid is annoyingly small and there are a lot of little plastic parts surely destined to be lost or thrown away. I also found it difficult to secure the lid before processing. The motor is adequate for most simple ice creams, sorbets, and yogurts, but it really strained to process a rich, custard-based ice cream. Save your money on this one.

The Cadillac of ice cream makers, the easiest and the most expensive machine available, is the electric self-contained freezer. First made in Italy, there are now several brands on the market, each one sleeker than its predecessor. If you've got serious money to invest in a machine, this little honey will crank out batch after batch of ice cream without so much as a groan. Because these models contain their own refrigeration unit, you pour the base mixture into a removable bowl and just turn the machine on. A full 1½ quarts of ice cream, frozen yogurt, or sorbet are produced in anywhere from 15 to 25 minutes, depending upon the manufacturer. These machines are getting less heavy and more compact as technology develops, but they still require a kitchen counter or other permanent place for storage. American manufacturers are presently hard at work trying to design affordable "ice cream clones" of these very elegant machines.

Glacée Glossary

Once you've made some of these fabulous ice creams and perhaps a topping or two, you'll probably begin to think more and more about presentation. They're just so much fun to serve. Aside from the fabulous assembled desserts presented in Chapter Five, here are some ice cream terms that may give you even more serving ideas.

An ice cream **bombe** is neither a failed recipe nor a potentially explosive dessert. It is simply ice cream, usually in at least two flavors, molded and served in a very grand manner. Make a Watermelon Bombe (page 00) for your Fourth of July party, and your guests will still be talking about it next Labor Day. Gourmet cookware shops and some well-stocked hardware stores often carry special hinged metal molds in a variety of shapes and sizes for making bombes. (I've also found terrific ones for next to nothing at garage sales and secondhand stores.) In lieu of a specialized mold, an ordinary mixing bowl will serve just as well to form a spectacular dome-shaped dessert.

One of the basic rules of cooking is if you ever need to bolster your self-esteem before serving a ridiculously simple dish, give it a French name. An ice cream **coupe** is simply a scoop of ice cream covered with fresh fruit or a fruit sauce, sometimes crowned with a cloud of whipped cream. A coupe is traditionally served in a footed glass with a wide bowl, similar to a saucer-type champagne glass, which is where the word comes from.

Sometimes a liquid dessert is just the ticket for casual occasions. An **ice cream**

float is as easy as it gets: ice cream is scooped into a tall, frosty glass and topped with a cold carbonated soft drink, such as root beer.

An **ice cream soda** is a mixture of fruit-flavored or chocolate syrup, ice cream, and sparkling soda water.

A **milkshake** is a blend of ice cream, cold milk, and a flavoring, such as fresh fruit or syrup.

A **malted** is a milk shake to which malted milk powder has been added.

A **parfait** consists of ice cream spooned into a tall, narrow, footed glass (like a tall champagne flute) and layered with sauces or fruits. Parfaits are often topped with whipped cream, a shower of chopped nuts, and a maraschino cherry. These towering striped beauties can be assembled hours in advance and kept frozen for instant entertaining. It's no accident *parfait* is the French word for perfect.

A **sundae** is one or more scoops of ice cream topped with sauce and/or fruit, nuts, and whipped cream. Sundaes range from the much-loved "black and white" scoop of vanilla topped with hot fudge sauce to the classically baroque banana split. Anything goes—from scoop to nuts—so have fun creating a month of sundaes. Stemmed tulip-shaped glasses are the container of choice for purists, but wine goblets or small glass bowls will do just fine.

When planning sundaes for a party or a make-your-own-sundae buffet, get a head start: form the ice cream balls up to 24 hours in advance. Scoop the ice cream onto a chilled baking sheet or pan. Freeze until the scoops are firm to the touch, about 30 minutes, and then cover well with plastic wrap and freeze until serving time.

Helpful Hints

Before you begin stockpiling all these frozen assets, here are a few helpful tips and facts to consider:

- Don't scrimp on the quality of the ingredients. Pure vanilla extract and fresh nuts will produce the ice cream you crave. Imitation flavors or stale ingredients won't do the trick.
- Ice creams made with cream and egg yolks are very smooth, reminiscent of the premium ice creams usually sold in small, pint-size containers. A custard base tends to stabilize the mixture and makes a softer ice cream than one without eggs.
- Ice creams made without eggs taste lighter and colder. They also freeze firmer than custard-based ice creams, making them harder to scoop.
- Chilling the ice cream base in the refrigerator prior to freezing allows time for the flavors to blend and ultimately produces a better-textured ice cream.
- Fill your ice cream machine no fuller than the manufacturer suggests. Some air must be incorporated, and ice cream needs room to expand while it freezes. This aeration, called overrun, improves the texture of the ice cream.
- Finished ice cream benefits from a few hours in the freezer to "ripen." During this time the mixture settles and the flavors blend. It also provides an opportunity for softer ice creams to firm up.
- Keep in mind that repeated thawing and refreezing encourages the formation of ice crystals and ruins the texture of the ice cream.

Now that you've got all the information you need for surefire success with lots of fun, let's get on with the big chill!

Chapter One
Make Mine Ice Cream

Remember when the most difficult decision in your life was choosing chocolate, vanilla, or strawberry? Needless to say, even though they remain perennially popular, we've come a long way from these voluptuous basics. Not only is premium ice cream readily available in nearly every town and in every flavor you can imagine, now we have affordable ice cream machines that will turn out a quart of dynamite ice cream at home in less than half an hour any time you have a hankering for it.

Making ice cream at home is a quick and easy procedure for even the inexperienced cook. The ingredients needed are few, and all are readily available at any supermarket. There are three very good reasons to make your own ice cream.

First, you have the opportunity to use the finest fresh, pure ingredients—unless you actually have a hankering for the cellulose gum, artificial flavors, annatto color, polysorbate 80, and whatever else that many commercial producers load into their ice cream. The second reason is that when you create it, you can choose any flavor you like, or even design a new one nobody ever made before. And the third reason is that if you're the cook, you get to lick the paddle when the ice cream is done.

This chapter contains all the standard favorites, like Voluptuous

Vanilla, Sensational Strawberry, and Classic Chocolate. For the more adventurous, there's Bittersweet Chocolate Truffle, Utterly Peanut Butter, Peppermint, and Caribbean Coconut. Whether you like your ice cream cold and icy or rich and custardy, there's a flavor here for you.

Vanilla Ice Cream

Ice creams made without eggs require no cooking. They have a fresh, somewhat icy texture that is less rich and creamy but simply delicious. They are also best eaten the same day.

Makes about 5 cups

---

2 cups heavy cream
2 cups half-and-half or light cream
¾ cup sugar
1 tablespoon vanilla extract

---

1. In a large bowl, combine the heavy cream and half-and-half. Gradually whisk in the sugar until blended.
2. Whisk in the vanilla. Refrigerate, covered, until very cold, at least 3 hours or as long as 3 days.
3. Whisk the mixture to blend and pour into the canister of an ice cream maker. Freeze according to the manufacturer's directions. Eat at once or transfer to a covered container and freeze up to 8 hours.

French Vanilla Ice Cream

This classic vanilla ice cream is the foundation for many other flavors, though it certainly needs no enhancement. Don't confuse its name with those ho-hum supermarket versions—there's nothing ordinary about this flavor. One lick, and you'll know why vanilla is still the most popular ice cream.

Makes about 5 cups

---

3 cups heavy cream
1 cup milk
¾ cup sugar

4 egg yolks
1 tablespoon vanilla extract

---

1. In a heavy medium saucepan, combine the cream, milk, and sugar. Cook over medium heat, stirring, until the sugar dissolves and the mixture is hot, 6 to 8 minutes.
2. Whisk the egg yolks in a medium bowl. Gradually whisk in about 1 cup of the warm cream. Return the egg mixture to the saucepan, reduce the heat to medium-low, and cook, stirring, until the custard thickens enough to coat the back of a spoon (at least 160°F. on a candy thermometer), 5 to 10 minutes. Do not boil or the egg yolks will curdle.
3. Strain the custard into a bowl and partially cover. Let cool 1 hour at room temperature. Stir in the vanilla. Refrigerate, covered, until very cold, at least 6 hours or as long as 3 days.
4. Pour the custard into the canister of an ice cream maker and freeze according to the manufacturer's directions. Transfer to a covered container and freeze at least 3 hours or as long as 3 days.

Speckled Vanilla Bean Ice Cream

Using whole vanilla beans instead of liquid extract makes this rich ice cream a vanilla lover's dream. Look for beans that are plump, moist, and pliable. Tiny black seeds, which look almost like powder, are released from the vanilla bean pods to make the specks that embellish the finished ice cream and lend it such a deep true vanilla flavor.

Makes about 5 cups

---

2 vanilla beans	¾ cup sugar
2 cups heavy cream	2 egg yolks
2 cups milk	

---

1. Using the pointed tip of a sharp knife, split the vanilla beans in half lengthwise and scrape the tiny black seeds into a heavy medium saucepan. Add the vanilla bean pods, cream, and milk and bring to a simmer over medium heat. Remove from the heat, cover, and let stand 30 minutes at room temperature to blend the flavors.

2. Add the sugar and cook over medium heat, stirring, until the sugar dissolves and the mixture is hot, 6 to 8 minutes.

3. Whisk the egg yolks in a medium bowl. Gradually whisk in about 1 cup of the warm vanilla cream. Return the egg mixture to the saucepan, reduce the heat to medium-low, and cook, stirring, until the custard thickens enough to coat the back of a spoon (at least 160°F. on a candy thermometer), 5 to 10 minutes. Do not boil or the egg yolks will curdle.

4. Strain the custard into a bowl, pressing through as many of the vanilla seeds as you can. Remove the vanilla bean pods from the strainer and add to the custard for flavor. Partially cover and let cool 1 hour at room temperature.

---

5. Refrigerate, covered, until very cold, at least 6 hours or as long as 3 days.

6. Discard the vanilla bean pods. Pour the custard into the canister of an ice cream maker and freeze according to the manufacturer's directions. Transfer to a covered container and freeze at least 3 hours or as long as 3 days.

Voluptuous Vanilla Ice Cream

I find vanilla's fragrance positively seductive and never tire of its flavor. This custard-based ice cream contains lighter cream but more egg yolks than French Vanilla (page 11), making it a lush variation on the same theme.

Makes about 5 cups

---

3 cups half-and-half or light cream
1 cup heavy cream
¾ cup sugar

6 egg yolks
1½ tablespoons vanilla extract

---

1. In a heavy medium saucepan, combine the half-and-half, heavy cream, and sugar. Cook over medium heat, stirring, until the sugar dissolves and the mixture is hot, 6 to 8 minutes.
2. Whisk the egg yolks in a medium bowl. Gradually whisk in about 1 cup of the warm cream. Return the egg mixture to the saucepan, reduce the heat to medium-low, and cook, stirring, until the custard thickens enough to coat the back of a spoon (at least 160°F. on a candy thermometer), 5 to 10 minutes. Do not boil or the egg yolks will curdle.
3. Strain the custard into a bowl and partially cover. Let cool 1 hour at room temperature. Stir in the vanilla. Refrigerate, covered, until very cold, at least 6 hours or as long as 3 days.
4. Pour the custard into the canister of an ice cream maker and freeze according to the manufacturer's directions. Transfer to a covered container and freeze at least 3 hours or as long as 3 days.

Honey Vanilla Ice Cream

Honey's silky texture and complex flavor makes a lovely ice cream. Experiment, using various types of honey, such as orange blossom, wildflower, or lavender.

Makes about 5 cups

---

1 cup heavy cream
3 cups half-and-half or light cream

½ cup honey
1 tablespoon vanilla extract

---

1. In a large bowl, combine the heavy cream and half-and-half. Gradually whisk in the honey to blend.
2. Whisk in the vanilla. Refrigerate, covered, until very cold, at least 3 hours or as long as 3 days.
3. Whisk the mixture to blend and pour into the canister of an ice cream maker. Freeze according to the manufacturer's directions. Eat at once or transfer to a covered container and freeze up to 8 hours.

Classic Chocolate Ice Cream

This is basic chocolate ice cream, pleasing by itself and versatile enough to blend with many other flavors.

Makes about 1½ quarts

---

2 cups heavy cream
2 cups half-and-half or light cream
¾ cup sugar
⅛ teaspoon salt

3 egg yolks
6 ounces bittersweet or semisweet choco-
    late, finely chopped
2 teaspoons vanilla extract

---

1. In a heavy saucepan, combine the heavy cream, half-and-half, sugar, and salt. Cook over medium heat, stirring, until the sugar dissolves and the mixture is hot, 6 to 8 minutes.
2. Whisk the egg yolks in a medium bowl. Gradually whisk in about 1 cup of the warm cream. Return the egg mixture to the saucepan, reduce the heat to medium-low, and cook, stirring, until the custard thickens enough to coat the back of a spoon (at least 160°F. on a candy thermometer), 5 to 10 minutes. Do not boil or the egg yolks will curdle. Remove from the heat. Immediately add the chocolate and stir until melted and smooth.
3. Strain the custard into a bowl and partially cover. Let cool 1 hour at room temperature. Stir in the vanilla. Refrigerate, covered, until very cold, at least 6 hours or as long as 3 days.
4. Pour the custard into the canister of an ice cream maker and freeze according to the manufacturer's directions. Transfer to a covered container and freeze at least 3 hours or as long as 3 days.

Simply Chocolate Ice Cream

There's more than one way to make ice cream for a chocolate lover. This version is less rich and even more easily made than Classic Chocolate Ice Cream (page 16), yet it still delivers a satisfying, velvety chocolate kick.

Makes about 5 cups

2 cups heavy cream
2 cups half-and-half or light cream
¾ cup sugar
Dash of salt

4 ounces bittersweet or semisweet chocolate, finely chopped
2 teaspoons vanilla extract

1. In a heavy saucepan, combine the heavy cream, half-and-half, sugar, and salt. Cook over medium heat, stirring, until the sugar dissolves and the mixture is hot, 6 to 8 minutes. Remove from the heat.
2. Immediately add the chocolate and stir until melted and smooth. Partially cover and let cool 30 minutes at room temperature. Stir in the vanilla. Refrigerate, covered, until very cold, at least 4 hours or as long as 3 days.
3. Pour into the canister of an ice cream maker and freeze according to the manufacturer's directions. Eat at once or transfer to a covered container and freeze up to 8 hours.

Bittersweet Chocolate Truffle Ice Cream

If you have been searching for the ultimate chocolate ice cream, look no further. This one is rich, dense, dark, and delicious. The tiny bit of salt, though not detectable, really boosts the chocolate flavor.

Makes about 1½ quarts

3 cups heavy cream
1 cup milk
1½ cups sugar
¼ cup unsweetened cocoa powder, preferably Dutch-process

⅛ teaspoon salt
4 egg yolks
4 (1-ounce) squares unsweetened chocolate, finely chopped
2 teaspoons vanilla extract

1. In a heavy saucepan, mix together the cream, milk, sugar, cocoa powder, and salt. Cook over medium heat, stirring, until the sugar dissolves and the mixture is hot, 6 to 8 minutes.
2. Whisk the egg yolks in a medium bowl. Gradually whisk in about 1 cup of the warm cocoa cream. Return the egg mixture to the saucepan, reduce the heat to medium-low, and cook, stirring, until the custard thickens enough to coat the back of a spoon (at least 160°F. on a candy thermometer), 5 to 10 minutes. Do not boil or the egg yolks will curdle. Remove from the heat. Immediately add the chocolate and stir until melted and smooth.
3. Strain the custard into a bowl and partially cover. Let cool 1 hour at room temperature. Stir in the vanilla. Refrigerate, covered, until very cold, at least 6 hours or as long as 3 days.
4. Pour the custard into the canister of an ice cream maker and freeze according to the manufacturer's directions. Transfer to a covered container and freeze at least 3 hours or as long as 3 days.

Chocolate Rum Ice Cream

This spirited ice cream is smooth as velvet and loaded with flavor. For variety, try a good brandy or Kentucky bourbon instead of rum. Remember that the addition of alcohol prevents ice cream from freezing solid.

Makes about 1½ quarts

---

3 cups heavy cream
1 cup half-and-half or light cream
¾ cup sugar
⅛ teaspoon salt

6 ounces bittersweet or semisweet chocolate, finely chopped
1 teaspoon vanilla extract
¼ cup dark rum

---

1. In a heavy saucepan, combine the heavy cream, half-and-half, sugar, and salt. Cook over medium heat, stirring, until the sugar dissolves and the mixture is hot, 6 to 8 minutes. Remove from the heat.

2. Immediately add the chocolate and stir until melted and smooth. Partially cover and let cool 30 minutes at room temperature. Stir in the vanilla. Refrigerate, covered, until very cold, at least 3 hours or as long as 3 days.

3. Whisk the mixture to blend and pour into the canister of an ice cream maker. Freeze according to the manufacturer's directions. When the ice cream is at the soft-serve stage, add the rum and process 1 minute longer. Eat at once or transfer to a covered container and freeze up to 8 hours.

Chocolate Brandy Alexander Ice Cream

Here's another way to enjoy an after-dinner drink. Instead of a glass, you use a spoon. This combination of liqueurs works beautifully with chocolate.

Makes about 1½ quarts

---

2 cups heavy cream
2 cups half-and-half or light cream
¾ cup sugar
⅛ teaspoon salt
6 ounces bittersweet or semisweet chocolate, finely chopped.

1 teaspoon vanilla extract
2 tablespoons brandy
2 tablespoons dark or white crème de cacao

---

1. In a heavy medium saucepan, combine the heavy cream, half-and-half, sugar, and salt. Cook over medium heat, stirring, until the sugar dissolves and the mixture is hot, 6 to 8 minutes. Remove from the heat.

2. Immediately add the chocolate and stir until melted and smooth. Partially cover and let cool 30 minutes at room temperature. Stir in the vanilla. Refrigerate, covered, until very cold, at least 3 hours or as long as 3 days.

3. Whisk the mixture to blend and pour into the canister of an ice cream maker. Freeze according to the manufacturer's directions. When the ice cream is at the soft-serve stage, add the brandy and crème de cacao and process 1 minute longer. Eat at once or transfer to a covered container and freeze up to 8 hours.

White Chocolate Ice Cream

White chocolate is cocoa butter without the dark brown chocolate "liquor." Imported brands of white chocolate are usually better quality, so use them whenever possible.

Makes about 5 cups

---

2 cups heavy cream
2 cups half-and-half or light cream
⅓ cup sugar

Dash of salt
8 ounces white chocolate, finely chopped
2 teaspoons vanilla extract

---

1. In a heavy medium saucepan, combine the heavy cream, half-and-half, sugar, and salt. Cook over medium heat, stirring, until the sugar dissolves and the mixture is hot, 6 to 8 minutes. Remove from the heat.

2. Immediately add the white chocolate and stir until melted and smooth. Partially cover and let cool 30 minutes at room temperature. Stir in the vanilla. Refrigerate, covered, until very cold, at least 3 hours or as long as 3 days.

3. Whisk the mixture to blend and pour into the canister of an ice cream maker. Freeze according to the manufacturer's directions. Eat at once or transfer to a covered container and freeze up to 8 hours.

Chocolate Malt Ice Cream

Most supermarkets stock malted milk powder on the same shelves as the mixes for chocolate milk and hot cocoa. For a double dose of malt flavor, try Chocolate Malt Ice Cream with Malt Balls (page 61).

Makes about 1½ quarts

---

2 cups heavy cream
2 cups milk
½ cup malted milk powder
⅓ cup sugar

Dash of salt
2 egg yolks
8 ounces milk chocolate, finely chopped
1 teaspoon vanilla extract

---

1. In a medium saucepan, combine the cream, milk, malted milk powder, sugar, and salt. Cook over medium heat, stirring, until the sugar dissolves and the mixture is well blended and hot, 6 to 8 minutes.

2. Whisk the egg yolks in a medium bowl. Gradually whisk in about 1 cup of the warm malted cream. Return the egg mixture to the saucepan, reduce the heat to medium-low, and cook, stirring, until the custard thickens enough to coat the back of a spoon (at least 160°F. on a candy thermometer), 5 to 10 minutes. Do not boil or the egg yolks will curdle. Remove from the heat.

3. Immediately add the chocolate and stir until melted and smooth. Strain the custard into a bowl and partially cover. Let cool 1 hour at room temperature. Stir in the vanilla. Refrigerate, covered, until very cold, at least 6 hours or as long as 3 days.

4. Pour the custard into the canister of an ice cream maker and freeze according to the manufacturer's directions. Transfer to a covered container and freeze at least 3 hours or as long as 3 days.

Mocha Ice Cream

The combination of coffee and chocolate is a universal favorite. Top each serving with a dollop of whipped cream and a chocolate-covered coffee bean; dust lightly with cocoa powder.

Makes about 1½ quarts

---

3 cups heavy cream
1 cup half-and-half or light cream
¾ cup sugar
1 tablespoon instant espresso powder

⅛ teaspoon salt
6 ounces bittersweet or semisweet chocolate, finely chopped
1 teaspoon vanilla extract

---

1. In a heavy saucepan, combine the heavy cream, half-and-half, sugar, espresso powder, and salt. Cook over medium heat, stirring, until the sugar dissolves and the mixture is hot, 6 to 8 minutes. Remove from the heat.

2. Immediately add the chocolate and stir until melted and smooth. Partially cover and let cool 30 minutes at room temperature. Stir in the vanilla. Refrigerate, covered, until very cold, at least 3 hours or as long as 3 days.

3. Whisk the mixture to blend and pour into the canister of an ice cream maker. Freeze according to the manufacturer's directions. Eat at once or transfer to a covered container and freeze up to 8 hours.

Creamy Coffee Ice Cream

Just imagine your morning cup of coffee with cream thickened and then frozen. Here you get the full coffee flavor without the added richness of egg custard.

Makes about 5 cups

---

2 tablespoons instant espresso powder
¼ cup boiling water
2 cups heavy cream

2 cups half-and-half or light cream
¾ cup sugar
2 teaspoons vanilla extract

---

1. In a large heatproof bowl, dissolve the espresso powder in the boiling water. Let cool.
2. Add the heavy cream and half-and-half to the cooled espresso. Gradually whisk in the sugar to blend. Whisk in the vanilla. Refrigerate, covered, until very cold, at least 3 hours or as long as 3 days.
3. Whisk the mixture to blend and pour into the canister of an ice cream maker. Freeze according to the manufacturer's directions. Eat at once or transfer to a covered container and freeze up to 8 hours.

Café au Lait Ice Cream

Don't let the fancy name fool you: it simply means coffee with milk. This is a mild coffee-flavored ice cream.

Makes about 5 cups

---

3 cups heavy cream	3 tablespoons instant coffee granules
1 cup milk	2 egg yolks
¾ cup sugar	2 teaspoons vanilla extract

---

1. In a heavy medium saucepan, combine the cream, milk, sugar, and instant coffee granules. Cook over medium heat, stirring, until the sugar and coffee granules dissolve and the mixture is hot, 6 to 8 minutes.

2. Whisk the egg yolks in a medium bowl. Gradually whisk in about 1 cup of the warm coffee cream. Return the egg mixture to the saucepan, reduce the heat to medium-low, and cook, stirring, until the custard thickens enough to coat the back of a spoon (at least 160°F. on a candy thermometer), 5 to 10 minutes. Do not boil or the egg yolks will curdle.

3. Strain the custard into a bowl and partially cover. Let cool 1 hour at room temperature. Stir in the vanilla. Refrigerate, covered, until very cold, at least 6 hours or as long as 3 days.

4. Pour the custard into the canister of an ice cream maker and freeze according to the manufacturer's directions. Transfer to a covered container and freeze at least 3 hours or as long as 3 days.

Espresso Bean Ice Cream

Even though I've never been a coffee drinker, I love the aroma of brewed coffee, and I adore the taste of coffee ice cream. Espresso adds the most depth of flavor and intensity. This recipe is reason enough for me to stand in line to buy freshly roasted beans.

Makes about 5 cups

---

2 ounces (about ⅔ cup) espresso or other
    dark roast coffee beans
2 cups heavy cream
2 cups milk

¾ cup sugar
2 egg yolks
2 teaspoons vanilla extract

---

1. Between 2 large sheets of parchment or wax paper, coarsely crack the coffee beans with a rolling pin or crush them under a heavy saucepan. (Do not grind the beans.)

2. Carefully lift the paper and pour the coffee bean pieces into a medium saucepan. Add the cream and milk and bring to a simmer over medium heat. Remove from the heat, cover, and let steep 30 minutes at room temperature.

3. Strain the espresso cream through a fine sieve into a bowl; discard the coffee beans. Return the cream to the saucepan and stir in the sugar. Cook over medium heat, stirring, until the sugar dissolves and the mixture is hot, 6 to 8 minutes.

4. Whisk the egg yolks in a medium bowl. Gradually whisk in about 1 cup of the warm espresso cream. Return the egg mixture to the saucepan, reduce the heat to medium-low, and cook, stirring, until the custard thickens enough to coat the back of a spoon (at least 160°F. on a candy thermometer), 5 to 10 minutes. Do not boil or the egg yolks will curdle.

5. Strain the custard into a bowl. Partially cover and let cool 1 hour at room temperature. Stir in the vanilla. Refrigerate, covered, until very cold, at least 6 hours or as long as 3 days.
6. Pour the custard into the canister of an ice cream maker and freeze according to the manufacturer's directions. Transfer to a covered container and freeze at least 3 hours or as long as 3 days.

Sensational Strawberry Ice Cream

When I was a child, strawberry was my very favorite ice cream flavor. It not only tasted sweet and fruity, it had the added bonus of being pink. I still think that's a big plus.

Makes about 1½ quarts

---

6 cups (3 pints) fresh strawberries, rinsed
 and hulled, or frozen unsweetened
 strawberries, thawed
1½ cups sugar

2 cups heavy cream
2 cups half-and-half or light cream
2 teaspoons vanilla extract

---

1. In a large bowl, mash the berries into a coarse puree. Stir in ¾ cup of the sugar. Let stand 1 hour.

2. Add the heavy cream, half-and-half, remaining ¾ cup sugar, and vanilla to the strawberries, stirring to mix and to dissolve the sugar. Refrigerate, covered, until very cold, at least 3 hours or as long as 2 days.

3. Stir the mixture to blend and pour into the canister of an ice cream maker. Freeze according to the manufacturer's directions. Eat at once or transfer to a covered container and freeze up to 8 hours.

Maple Walnut Ice Cream

This is no time to scrimp on ingredients; be sure to use only pure maple syrup. The imitation stuff lacks body and tastes artificial.

Makes about 1½ quarts

---

1 cup coarsely chopped walnuts (about
    4 ounces)
2 cups heavy cream
2 cups half-and-half or light cream

¾ cup maple syrup
¼ cup sugar
⅛ teaspoon salt
1½ teaspoons vanilla extract

---

1. Preheat the oven to 325°F. Spread out the walnuts on a baking sheet and toast in the oven, shaking the pan several times, until lightly browned, 5 to 8 minutes. Transfer the nuts to a dish and let cool.

2. In a large bowl, combine the heavy cream and half-and-half. Add the maple syrup, sugar, salt, and vanilla. Whisk to blend well. Refrigerate, covered, until very cold, at least 3 hours or as long as 3 days.

3. Whisk the mixture to blend and pour into the canister of an ice cream maker. Freeze according to the manufacturer's directions. When the ice cream is at the soft-serve stage, add the toasted walnuts and process 1 minute longer. Eat at once or transfer to a covered container and freeze up to 8 hours.

Butter Pecan Ice Cream

Buttery toasted nuts transform vanilla ice cream into a voluptuous new flavor. Nuts should be stored in the freezer so they do not turn rancid. Sample the nuts before you toast them just to be sure they are fresh tasting.

Makes about 1½ quarts

---

4 tablespoons unsalted butter, cut into
    4 or more pieces
1 cup pecan halves and pieces (about
    4 ounces)
¼ teaspoon salt

2 cups heavy cream
2 cups half-and-half or light cream
¾ cup sugar
2 egg yolks
2 teaspoons vanilla extract

---

1. In a medium skillet, melt the butter over low heat. Add the pecans and salt. Cook, stirring, until the pecans are crisp and just beginning to brown, about 5 minutes. Remove from the heat. Using a slotted spoon, lift out the pecans and let cool. Reserve the melted butter in the pan.

2. In a heavy medium saucepan, combine the heavy cream, half-and-half, and sugar. Cook over medium heat, stirring, until the sugar dissolves and the mixture is hot, 6 to 8 minutes.

3. Whisk the egg yolks in a medium bowl. Gradually whisk in about 1 cup of the warm cream. Return the egg mixture to the saucepan, reduce the heat to medium-low, and cook, stirring, until the custard thickens enough to coat the back of a spoon (at least 160°F. on a candy thermometer), 5 to 10 minutes. Do not boil or the egg yolks will curdle.

4. Strain the custard into a bowl. Stir in the reserved melted butter. Partially cover and let cool 1 hour at room temperature. Stir in the vanilla. Refrigerate, covered, until very cold, at least 6 hours or as long as 3 days.

---

5. Pour the custard into the canister of an ice cream maker and freeze according to the manufacturer's directions. When the ice cream is at the soft-serve stage, add the pecans and process 1 minute longer. Transfer to a covered container and freeze at least 3 hours or as long as 3 days.

Pistachio Ice Cream

Purists may opt for a natural white ice cream, but to me, pistachio isn't pistachio without a few drops of green food coloring.

Makes about 1½ quarts

---

2 cups heavy cream
2 cups half-and-half or light cream
¾ cup sugar
1 teaspoon vanilla extract

1 teaspoon almond extract
2 to 3 drops green food coloring
(optional)
1 cup shelled unsalted pistachio nuts

---

1. Preheat the oven to 325°F. In a large bowl, combine the heavy cream and half-and-half. Gradually whisk in the sugar to blend.

2. Stir in the vanilla, almond extract, and green food coloring to blend well. Refrigerate, covered, until very cold, at least 3 hours or as long as 3 days.

3. Spread out the pistachios on a baking sheet. Toast in the oven, shaking the pan several times, until the nuts are lightly browned and the skins are cracked, 5 to 8 minutes. Rub the warm nuts in a terrycloth towel to remove as much skin as possible. Let cool, then chop coarsely.

4. Whisk the cream base to blend and pour into the canister of an ice cream maker. Freeze according to the manufacturer's directions. When the ice cream is at the soft-serve stage, add the chopped pistachios and process 1 minute longer. Eat at once or transfer to a covered container and freeze up to 8 hours.

Rocky Road Ice Cream

This is another childhood favorite that still tastes pretty darn good. Be sure to take the extra step of toasting the nuts; it gives them added flavor as well as crunch.

Makes about 1½ quarts

3 cups heavy cream
1 cup half-and-half or light cream
¾ cup sugar
⅛ teaspoon salt
6 ounces bittersweet or semisweet chocolate, finely chopped

2 teaspoons vanilla extract
½ cup coarsely chopped walnuts (about 2 ounces)
1 cup miniature marshmallows (about 2 ounces)

1. In a heavy medium saucepan, combine the heavy cream, half-and-half, sugar, and salt. Cook over medium heat, stirring, until the sugar dissolves and the mixture is hot, 6 to 8 minutes. Remove from the heat.

2. Immediately add the chocolate and stir until melted and smooth. Partially cover and let cool 30 minutes at room temperature. Stir in the vanilla. Refrigerate, covered, until very cold, at least 3 hours or as long as 3 days.

3. Preheat the oven to 325°F. Spread the walnuts on a baking sheet and toast in the oven, shaking the pan several times, until lightly browned, 5 to 8 minutes. Let cool.

4. Whisk the mixture to blend and pour into the canister of an ice cream maker. Freeze according to the manufacturer's directions. When the ice cream is at the soft-serve stage, add the toasted walnuts and the marshmallows and process 1 minute longer. Eat at once or transfer to a covered container and freeze up to 8 hours.

Peaches 'n' Cream Ice Cream

When fragrant, tree-ripened peaches are not available, unsweetened frozen peach slices are a good alternative. This recipe also works well using a combination of stone fruits, such as peaches, nectarines, and apricots.

Makes about 1½ quarts

---

6 medium peaches (about 2 pounds), peeled and stoned, or 4 cups frozen unsweetened peach slices, thawed
1 cup sugar

3 cups heavy cream
1 cup milk
2 teaspoons vanilla extract

---

1. In a large bowl, mash the peaches into a coarse puree. Stir in ¼ cup of the sugar. Let stand 1 hour.

2. Add the cream, milk, remaining ¾ cup sugar, and vanilla to peaches, stirring to blend. Refrigerate, covered, until very cold, at least 3 hours or as long as 3 days.

3. Stir the mixture to blend and pour into the canister of an ice cream maker. Freeze according to the manufacturer's directions. Eat at once or transfer to a covered container and freeze up to 8 hours.

Raspberries 'n' Cream Ice Cream

Use fresh raspberries when you can pick them yourself or when you find them for a good price at the farmers' market. Otherwise, frozen berries are fine. Feel free to substitute blackberries or boysenberries, but be sure to adjust the amount of sugar in the recipe according to the sweetness of the fruit.

Makes about 1½ quarts

---

4 cups (2 pints) fresh raspberries or frozen unsweetened raspberries
1½ cups sugar
2 cups heavy cream

2 cups milk
1 teaspoon vanilla extract or ¼ teaspoon almond extract

---

1. If using fresh berries, rinse gently and drain in a colander. Pick over to remove any badly bruised or moldy fruit.

2. Place the berries in a heavy nonreactive medium saucepan. Cook over medium heat, crushing the berries with the back of a spoon, until they exude most of their juice, 2 to 3 minutes.

3. Add the sugar and cook, stirring, until the sugar dissolves and a light syrup forms, 3 to 5 minutes. Strain the berries and syrup into a bowl, pressing through as much of the juice and fruit as you can.

4. Stir the cream, milk, and vanilla into the berry base. Cover and refrigerate until very cold, at least 4 hours or as long as 2 days.

5. Stir the mixture to blend and pour into the canister of an ice cream maker. Freeze according to the manufacturer's directions. Eat at once or transfer to a covered container and freeze up to 8 hours.

Lemon Custard Ice Cream

The yellow outer skin of a lemon, called the zest, contains aromatic oils, which best convey its distinct sweet-tart flavor. This tartness is a perfect foil to rich custard ice cream.

Makes about 1½ quarts

---

6 medium lemons (about 1½ pounds)
1⅓ cups sugar
2 cups heavy cream

2 cups milk
2 egg yolks
1½ teaspoons vanilla extract

---

1. Using a vegetable brush and warm water, wash the lemons well; pat dry. Using a swivel-bladed vegetable peeler, remove only the yellow zest of the lemon skins, not the bitter white pith. In a food processor, combine the strips of lemon zest with ⅓ cup of the sugar. Process until the zest is finely minced, about 30 seconds.

2. In a heavy medium nonreactive saucepan, combine the minced lemon zest and sugar with the remaining 1 cup sugar, the cream, and the milk. Cook over medium heat, stirring, until the sugar dissolves and the mixture is hot, 6 to 8 minutes.

3. Whisk the egg yolks in a medium bowl. Gradually whisk in about 1 cup of the warm lemon cream. Return to the saucepan, reduce the heat to medium-low, and cook, stirring, until the custard thickens enough to coat the back of a spoon (at least 160°F. on a candy thermometer), 5 to 10 minutes. Do not boil or the egg yolks will curdle. Pour into a bowl and partially cover. Let cool 1 hour at room temperature.

4. Squeeze ¾ cup juice from the lemons, discarding any seeds. Add the lemon juice and vanilla to the custard, stirring to blend. Refrigerate, covered, until very cold, at least 6 hours or as long as 3 days.

5. Stir the lemon custard and pour into the canister of an ice cream maker. Freeze according to the manufacturer's directions. Transfer to a covered container and freeze at least 3 hours or as long as 3 days.

Utterly Peanut Butter Ice Cream

If you're sneering at the very idea of this, uncurl that upper lip and give it a try. The creamy texture of peanut butter combined with its subtle yet distinct flavor make this surprisingly pleasing. Be sure to use a standard commercial brand of peanut butter; the "natural" and "old-fashioned" ones tend to separate.

Makes about 1½ quarts

---

2 cups heavy cream

2 cups milk

¾ cup sugar

1 cup (packed) creamy peanut butter

2 egg yolks

2 teaspoons vanilla extract

---

1. In a heavy medium saucepan, combine the cream, milk, and sugar. Cook over medium heat, stirring, until the sugar dissolves and the mixture is hot, 6 to 8 minutes.

2. Gradually mix in the peanut butter by large spoonfuls, stirring well after each addition, until the peanut butter has melted and the mixture is smooth.

3. Whisk the egg yolks in a medium bowl. Gradually whisk in about 1 cup of the warm peanut butter cream. Return the egg mixture to the saucepan, reduce the heat to medium-low, and cook, stirring, until the custard thickens enough to coat the back of a spoon (at least 160°F. on a candy thermometer), 5 to 10 minutes. Do not boil or the egg yolks will curdle.

4. Strain the custard into a bowl and partially cover. Let cool 1 hour at room temperature. Stir in the vanilla. Refrigerate, covered, until very cold, at least 6 hours or as long as 3 days.

5. Pour the custard into the canister of an ice cream maker and freeze according to the manufacturer's directions. Transfer to a covered container and freeze at least 3 hours or as long as 3 days.

Coconut Ice Cream with Chocolate and Roasted Almonds

Preston's Candies and Ice Cream of Burlingame, California, makes superior sweets in the time-honored tradition. This is my version of one of their inspired ice cream flavors.

Makes about 1½ quarts

---

2 cups heavy cream
2 cups milk
1 (7-ounce) package sweetened flaked or shredded coconut
½ cup sugar
2 egg yolks
2 teaspoons vanilla extract

¼ teaspoon almond extract
¾ cup coarsely chopped bittersweet or semi-sweet chocolate (4 ounces)
¾ cup roasted whole salted or unsalted almonds (about 4 ounces), very coarsely chopped

---

1. In a heavy medium saucepan, combine the cream, milk, and 1 cup of the coconut. Bring to a simmer over medium heat. Remove from the heat, cover, and let stand 30 minutes at room temperature.

2. Strain the cream mixture through a sieve into a bowl, pressing to extract as much liquid as possible; discard the coconut. Return the coconut cream to the saucepan and stir in the sugar. Cook over medium heat, stirring, until the sugar dissolves and the mixture is hot, 6 to 8 minutes.

3. Whisk the egg yolks in a medium bowl. Gradually whisk in about 1 cup of the warm cream. Return the egg mixture to the saucepan, reduce the heat to medium-low, and cook, stirring, until the custard thickens enough to coat the back of a spoon (at least 160°F. on a candy thermometer), 5 to 10 minutes. Do not boil or the egg yolks will curdle.

4. Strain the custard into a bowl and partially cover. Let cool 1 hour at room temperature. Stir in the vanilla and almond extracts. Refrigerate, covered, until very cold, at least 6 hours or as long as 3 days.

5. Pour the custard into the canister of an ice cream maker and freeze according to the manufacturer's directions. When the ice cream is at the soft-serve stage, add the remaining coconut, the chocolate, and the almonds and process 1 to 2 minutes longer. Transfer to a covered container and freeze at least 3 hours or as long as 3 days.

Caribbean Coconut Ice Cream

Makes about 1½ quarts

---

2 cups heavy cream

2 cups milk

1 (7-ounce) package sweetened flaked or
    shredded coconut

½ cup sugar

¼ teaspoon grated nutmeg

⅛ teaspoon ground cinnamon

2 egg yolks

2 teaspoons vanilla extract

---

1. In a heavy medium saucepan, combine the cream, milk, and 1 cup of the coconut. Bring to a simmer over medium heat. Remove from the heat, cover, and let stand 30 minutes at room temperature.

2. Strain the cream mixture through a sieve into a bowl, pressing to extract as much liquid as possible; discard the coconut. Return the coconut cream to the saucepan. Stir in the sugar, nutmeg, and cinnamon. Cook over medium heat, stirring, until the sugar dissolves and the mixture is hot, 6 to 8 minutes.

3. Whisk the egg yolks in a medium bowl. Gradually whisk in about 1 cup of the warm coconut cream. Return the egg mixture to the saucepan, reduce the heat to medium-low, and cook, stirring, until the custard thickens enough to coat the back of a spoon. (at least 160°F. on a candy thermomenter), 5 to 10 minutes. Do not boil or the egg yolks will curdle.

4. Strain the custard into a bowl and partially cover. Let cool 1 hour at room temperature. Stir in the vanilla. Refrigerate, covered, until very cold, at least 6 hours or as long as 3 days.

5. Pour the custard into the canister of an ice cream maker and freezr according to the manufacturer's directions. When the ice cream is at the soft-serve stage, add the remaining coconut and process 1 minute longer. Transfer to a covered container and freeze at least 3 hours or as long as 3 days.

Cinnamon Ice Cream

Try a scoop of this sweetly spiced ice cream for a jazzy apple pie à la mode or as an accompaniment to sliced fresh peaches or pears. Just before serving, garnish with a light dusting of ground cinnamon.

Makes about 5 cups

---

2 cups heavy cream	¾ cup sugar
2 cups milk	3 egg yolks
1 (3-inch) cinnamon stick	1 teaspoon ground cinnamon
1 (2-inch) strip of lemon zest	1½ teaspoons vanilla extract

---

1. In a heavy saucepan, combine the cream, milk, cinnamon stick, and lemon zest. Bring to a simmer over medium heat. Remove from the heat, cover, and let stand 30 minutes at room temperature.

2. Discard the cinnamon stick and lemon zest. Add the sugar and cook over medium heat, stirring, until the sugar dissolves and the mixture is hot, 6 to 8 minutes.

3. Whisk the egg yolks in a medium bowl. Gradually whisk in about 1 cup of the warm cinnamon cream. Return the egg mixture to the saucepan, reduce the heat to medium-low, and cook, stirring, until the custard thickens enough to coat the back of a spoon (at least 160°F. on a candy thermometer), 5 to 10 minutes. Do not boil or the egg yolks will curdle.

4. Strain the custard into a bowl. Stir in the ground cinnamon. Partially cover and let cool 1 hour at room temperature. Stir in the vanilla. Refrigerate, covered, until very cold, at least 6 hours or as long as 3 days.

5. Pour the custard into the canister of an ice cream maker and freeze according to the manufacturer's directions. Transfer to a covered container and freeze at least 3 hours or as long as 3 days.

Double Ginger Ice Cream

Preserved stem ginger comes in attractive 14-ounce crocks that are available at most Asian markets as well as in many supermarkets and specialty food shops. This sweet and spicy ice cream is a natural conclusion to any Asian meal. It can be served alone, with fresh fruit, or drizzled with Chocolate Ginger Sauce (page 87). Just don't forget the fortune cookies!

Makes about 5 cups

---

6 ounces fresh ginger
2 cups heavy cream
2 cups milk
1 (2-inch) strip of lemon zest
½ cup sugar
2 egg yolks

½ cup finely chopped preserved stem ginger
3 tablespoons syrup from the jar of preserved ginger
2 teaspoons vanilla extract

---

1. Peel the ginger with a swivel-bladed vegetable peeler and cut into slices about ¼ inch thick. (There should be about 1 cup.) Place the ginger in a small nonreactive saucepan and add water to cover. Bring to a boil over medium-high heat. Boil 30 seconds, then remove from the heat and drain in a colander.

2. In a heavy medium saucepan, combine the ginger slices, cream, milk, and lemon zest. Bring to a simmer over medium heat. Remove from the heat, cover, and let stand 1 hour at room temperature.

3. Using a slotted spoon, remove and discard the ginger slices and lemon zest. Add the sugar to the cream mixture and cook over medium heat, stirring, until the sugar dissolves and the mixture is hot, 6 to 8 minutes.

4. Whisk the egg yolks in a medium bowl. Gradually whisk in about 1 cup of the warm ginger cream. Return the egg mixture to the saucepan, reduce the heat to medium-low, and cook, stirring, until the custard thickens enough to coat the back of a spoon (at least 160°F. on a candy thermometer), 5 to 10 minutes. Do not boil or the egg yolks will curdle.

5. Strain the custard into a bowl. Partially cover and let cool 1 hour at room temperature Stir in the stem ginger, ginger syrup, and vanilla. Refrigerate, covered, at least 6 hours or as long as 3 days.

6. Stir the custard to distribute the ginger evenly. Pour into the canister of an ice cream maker and freeze according to the manufacturer's directions. Transfer to a covered container and freeze at least 3 hours or as long as 3 days.

Brown Sugar Ice Cream

Brown sugar imparts a golden color and rich caramel flavor to this ice cream. When you "feel like a nut," try Brown Sugar Ice Cream with Toasted Almonds and Amaretto (page 72).

Makes about 5 cups

---

3 cups heavy cream
1 cup half-and-half or light cream
1 cup (packed) light or dark brown sugar
1 tablespoon vanilla extract

---

1. In a large bowl, combine the heavy cream and half-and-half. Gradually whisk in the brown sugar to blend.
2. Whisk in the vanilla. Refrigerate, covered, until very cold, at least 3 hours or as long as 3 days.
3. Whisk the mixture to blend and pour into the canister of an ice cream maker. Freeze according to the manufacturer's directions. Eat at once or transfer to a covered container and freeze up to 8 hours.

Rum Raisin Ice Cream

This was probably the first flavor of commercially produced premium ice cream I ever tasted. Now I make it at home, using the best quality rum and, just for fun, a combination of dark and golden raisins.

Makes about 1½ quarts

¾ cup raisins, preferably half dark and half
    golden (about 6 ounces)
About ¾ cup dark rum
3 cups heavy cream

1 cup half-and-half or light cream
¾ cup sugar
1 teaspoon vanilla extract

---

1. In a small nonreactive saucepan, combine the raisins with enough rum to cover. Bring to a simmer over low heat. (Watch carefully. If the alcohol gets too hot, it will ignite.) Remove from the heat and let cool. Strain the rum into a heatproof glass measuring cup and set aside. Reserve the raisins.

2. In a large bowl, combine the heavy cream and half-and-half. Gradually whisk in the sugar to blend. Whisk in the vanilla. Refrigerate, covered, until very cold, at least 3 hours or as long as 3 days.

3. Whisk the mixture to blend and pour into the canister of an ice cream maker. Freeze according to the manufacturer's directions. When the ice cream is at the soft-serve stage, add ⅓ cup of the rum and the raisins and process 1 minute longer. (Discard any remaining rum or reserve for another use.) Eat at once or transfer to a covered container and freeze up to 8 hours.

Prune and Armagnac Ice Cream

A warm bath in fine French brandy elevates the humble prune to regal heights. Although I probably wouldn't serve it to a troop of Boy Scouts, this rich and boozy combo is a delicious surprise to most adult palates.

Makes about 1½ quarts

---

3 cups heavy cream
1 cup milk
¾ cup sugar
4 egg yolks
¾ cup coarsely chopped pitted prunes
   (about 6 ounces)

About ¾ cup Armagnac, Cognac, or other
   very good brandy
1 teaspoon vanilla extract

---

1. In a heavy medium saucepan, combine the cream, milk, and sugar. Cook over medium heat, stirring, until the sugar dissolves and the mixture is hot, 6 to 8 minutes.

2. Whisk the egg yolks in a medium bowl. Gradually whisk in about 1 cup of the warm cream. Return the egg mixture to the saucepan, reduce the heat to medium-low, and cook, stirring, until the custard thickens enough to coat the back of a spoon (at least 160°F. on a candy thermometer), 5 to 10 minutes. Do not boil or the egg yolks will curdle.

3. Strain the custard into a bowl and partially cover. Let cool 1 hour at room temperature.

4. Put the prunes in a small nonreactive saucepan. Add enough Armagnac to cover. Warm over low heat just until hot. (Do not bring to a simmer; if the alcohol gets too hot it will ignite.) Remove from the heat and let cool. Strain the Armagnac into a heatproof glass measuring cup and set aside. Reserve the prunes.

5. Stir ½ cup of the Armagnac and the vanilla into the cooled custard. (Discard any remaining Armagnac or reserve for another use.) Refrigerate, covered, until very cold, at least 6 hours or as long as 3 days.

6. Pour the custard into the canister of an ice cream maker and freeze according to the manufacturer's directions. When the ice cream is at the soft-serve stage, add the prunes and process 1 minute longer. Transfer to a covered container and freeze at least 3 hours or as long as 3 days.

Pumpkin Pie Ice Cream

Makes about 1½ quarts

2 cups heavy cream
2 cups milk
¾ cup (packed) light or dark brown sugar
¼ cup granulated sugar
3 egg yolks
1 cup canned solid-pack unsweetened
  pumpkin

1 tablespoon vanilla extract
1 teaspoon ground cinnamon
½ teaspoon ground ginger
¼ teaspoon grated fresh nutmeg or
  ground nutmeg
⅛ teaspoon ground cloves
⅛ teaspoon salt

1. In a heavy medium saucepan, combine the cream, milk, brown sugar, and granulated sugar. Cook over medium heat, stirring, until the sugars dissolve and the mixture is hot, 5 to 7 minutes.
2. Whisk the egg yolks in a medium bowl. Gradually whisk in about 1 cup of the warm cream. Return the egg mixture to the saucepan, reduce the heat to medium-low, and cook, stirring, until the custard thickens enough to coat the back of a spoon (at least 160°F. on a candy thermometer), 5 to 10 minutes. Do not boil or the egg yolks will curdle.
3. Strain the custard into a bowl and partially cover. Let cool 1 hour at room temperature. In a medium bowl, combine the pumpkin, vanilla, cinnamon, ginger, nutmeg, cloves, and salt. Blend well. Add to the custard and stir to mix evenly. Refrigerate, covered, until very cold, at least 6 hours or as long as 3 days.
4. Stir the pumpkin custard and pour into the canister of an ice cream maker. Freeze according to the manufacturer's directions. Transfer to a covered container and freeze at least 3 hours or as long as 3 days.

Eggnog Ice Cream

It's a shame to reserve this flavor for the month of December only. You may want to dust off that old punch bowl set packed away in your cupboard and serve scoops of this in the little glass cups, grating a bit more fresh nutmeg on top. If you're serving children, feel free to omit the alcohol from the recipe.

Makes about 5 cups

---

3 cups heavy cream
1 cup milk
¾ cup sugar
4 egg yolks
2 teaspoons vanilla extract

1 teaspoon grated fresh nutmeg or ½ teaspoon ground nutmeg
3 tablespoons brandy or bourbon
3 tablespoons dark rum

---

1. In a heavy medium saucepan, combine the cream, milk, and sugar. Cook over medium heat, stirring, until the sugar dissolves and the mixture is hot, 6 to 8 minutes.

2. Whisk the egg yolks in a medium bowl. Gradually whisk in about 1 cup of the warm cream. Return the egg mixture to the saucepan, reduce the heat to medium-low, and cook, stirring, until the custard thickens enough to coat the back of a spoon (at least 160°F. on a candy thermometer), 5 to 10 minutes. Do not boil or the egg yolks will curdle.

3. Strain the custard into a bowl and partially cover. Let cool 1 hour at room temperature. Stir in the vanilla and nutmeg. Refrigerate, covered, until very cold, at least 6 hours or as long as 3 days.

4. Pour the custard into the canister of an ice cream maker and freeze according to the manufacturer's directions. When the mixture is at the soft-serve stage, add the brandy and rum and process 1 minute longer. Transfer to a covered container and freeze at least 3 hours or as long as 3 days.

Peppermint Ice Cream

If peppermint sticks are difficult to find, hard peppermint candies will also do the trick. Since both types of candy are usually sold individually wrapped in cellophane, they can be crushed easily under a heavy pot before unwrapping.

Makes about 1½ quarts

---

2 cups heavy cream
2 cups milk
¾ cup crushed peppermint stick candy
  (about 6 ounces)

⅔ cup sugar
2 egg yolks
1½ teaspoons vanilla extract
½ teaspoon peppermint extract

---

1. In a heavy medium saucepan, combine the cream, milk, ¼ cup of the crushed peppermint candy, and the sugar. Cook over medium heat, stirring, until the sugar and candy dissolve and the mixture is hot, 6 to 8 minutes.

2. Whisk the egg yolks in a medium bowl. Gradually whisk in about 1 cup of the warm cream. Return the egg mixture to the saucepan, reduce the heat to medium-low, and cook, stirring, until the custard thickens enough to coat the back of a spoon (at least 160°F. on a candy thermometer), 5 to 10 minutes. Do not boil or the egg yolks will curdle.

3. Strain the custard into a bowl and partially cover. Let cool 1 hour at room temperature. Stir in the vanilla and peppermint extracts. Refrigerate, covered, until very cold, at least 6 hours or as long as 3 days.

4. Pour the custard into the canister of an ice cream maker and freeze according to the manufacturer's directions. When the ice cream is at the soft-serve stage, add the remaining ½ cup crushed peppermint candy and process 1 minute longer. Transfer to a covered container and freeze at last 3 hours or as long as 3 days.

Grasshopper Ice Cream

There's no need to tell children this flavor is based on the after-dinner drink made popular in the '50s; if you can convince them it contains actual grasshoppers, maybe then they won't feel slighted it's not for them. I serve scoops of this pale green potion in stemmed martini glasses, just like grown-ups do.

Makes about 5 cups

---

2 cups heavy cream
2 cups half-and-half or light cream
¾ cup sugar

1 teaspoon vanilla extract
2 tablespoons green crème de menthe
2 tablespoons white crème de cacao

---

1. In a large bowl, combine the heavy cream and half-and-half. Gradually whisk in the sugar to blend.

2. Whisk in the vanilla. Refrigerate, covered, until very cold, at least 3 hours or as long as 3 days.

3. Whisk the mixture to blend and pour into the canister of an ice cream maker. Freeze according to the manufacturer's directions. When the ice cream is at the soft-serve stage, add the crème de menthe and crème de cacao and process 1 minute longer. Eat at once or transfer to a covered container and freeze up to 8 hours.

Chapter Two
Swirls and Twirls

Walk down the frozen foods aisle of any supermarket and you will be amazed at the assortment of ice creams featuring imaginative swirls, ripples, and add-ins. Now you can make them yourself in your kitchen ice cream parlor, at a fraction of the cost of premium store-bought.

This chapter is filled with ways to stretch your creativity to its limits. Now that you've mastered all the basic flavors (and then some), have fun creating your own personalized flavors by incorporating additional sweet and crunchy textures. Whether you're partial to chocolate, fruit, nuts, caramel, or cream, you'll find a delicious extra layer of flavor to twirl right into the ice cream base. Other recipes offer sauces and crunchies to top it all off.

Just to get you started on this odyssey, there's Chunky Peanut Fudge Ripple and Brown Sugar with Toasted Almonds and Amaretto. Flavors like Candy Crunch, Cherries 'n' Chocolate, and Vanilla Cookie Dough are sure to appeal to children big and little. Truffled Espresso Bean, Chocolate Rum with Candied Chestnuts, and Eggnog Cranberry Swirl are very grown-up flavors with a sophisticated flair, ideal for holiday entertaining or for other special occasions at home.

To get you dreaming about homemade sundaes and parfaits, there are easy recipes for silky sauces designed to complement all your prized ice creams. Sample the array of chocolate sauces, from the basic Homemade Chocolate Syrup to Hot Brandied Fudge Sauce. Smooth and luscious

Best Butterscotch Sauce and its variations will give you the leading edge on creating some of the tastiest desserts around.

And if too much is never enough, pile on the garnishes! Crisp little Chocolate Leaves, crackling sweet Caramel Icicles, and a shower of Chocolate Curls and Twirls will bring professional flair to your homemade desserts. And just like ice cream, these can be made conveniently in advance.

Chipper Chocolate Ice Cream

Chocolate chips are one of the most familiar and simplest add-ins. For this recipe I've used a colorful assortment of chips for a flurry of flavor.

Makes about 1¾ quarts

½ cup semisweet chocolate chips
½ cup white chocolate chips, vanilla milk chips, or classic white chips
½ cup naturally flavored peanut butter chips
1 recipe Classic Chocolate Ice Cream (page 16)

---

1. In a small bowl, toss the semisweet and white chocolate chips with the peanut butter chips. Cover and refrigerate until needed.

2. Prepare Classic Chocolate Ice Cream through step 3. Pour the custard into the canister of an ice cream maker and freeze according to the manufacturer's directions.

3. When the ice cream is at the soft-serve stage, add the cold chips and process 1 minute longer. Transfer to a covered container and freeze at least 3 hours or as long as 3 days.

Cherries 'n' Chocolate Ice Cream

With this recipe I pay homage to the high priests of ice cream who gave the world Cherry Garcia. Bless you, Ben & Jerry.

Makes about 1½ quarts

½ pound fresh sweet cherries or 1 cup frozen unsweetened Bing cherries, thawed
2 tablespoons sugar
2 ounces bittersweet or semisweet chocolate, well chilled
1 recipe French Vanilla Ice Cream (page 11)

---

1. If using fresh cherries, remove any stems. Rinse well and pat dry with paper towels. Working over a bowl to catch the juices, cut the cherries in half with a small stainless steel knife. Cut out the pit with the tip of the knife and drop the cherries into the bowl.
2. Add the sugar to the cherries and stir to mix evenly. Cover and refrigerate until needed.
3. Using the large holes on a hand grater, coarsely grate the cold chocolate. Place in a small bowl, cover, and refrigerate until needed.
4. Prepare French Vanilla Ice Cream through step 3. Pour the custard into the canister of an ice cream maker and freeze according to the manufacturer's directions.
5. When the ice cream is at the soft-serve stage, add the cold cherries and their juices and then the chocolate. Process 1 minute longer. Transfer to a covered container and freeze at least 3 hours or as long as 3 days.

Chocolate Truffle Ice Cream with Marshmallow Swirl

Just when you thought Bittersweet Chocolate Truffle Ice Cream couldn't get any better, here's an added fillip.

Makes about 1³/₄ quarts

---

1 recipe Bittersweet Chocolate Truffle Ice Cream (page 18)
1 (7-ounce) jar marshmallow cream
3 tablespoons water

---

1. Prepare Bittersweet Chocolate Truffle Ice Cream through step 3. Pour the custard into the canister of an ice cream maker and freeze according to the manufacturer's directions.
2. In a small saucepan, melt the marshmallow cream over low heat. Stir in the water until well blended. Remove from the heat and let cool slightly, at least 10 minutes.
3. When the ice cream mixture is at the soft-serve stage, add the marshmallow cream and process just until swirled throughout, 30 to 60 seconds. Transfer to a covered container and freeze at least 3 hours or as long as 3 days.

Chocolate Peanut Butter Cup Ice Cream

Chocolate and peanut butter are natural companions, brought to a blissful marriage in cup candies. Here the popular confections are added to chocolate ice cream to produce a frozen delight of which dreams are made.

Makes about 1½ quarts

---

3 (1.8-ounce) packages peanut butter cups (2 per package), such as Reese's
1 recipe Classic Chocolate Ice Cream (page 16)

---

1. Chop the peanut butter cups into ¾-inch pieces. (There will be about 1 cup.) Cover and refrigerate until needed.
2. Prepare Classic Chocolate Ice Cream through step 3. Pour the custard into the canister of an ice cream maker and freeze according to the manufacturer's directions.
3. When the ice cream is at the soft-serve stage, add the cold peanut butter cup pieces and process 1 minute longer. Transfer to a covered container and freeze for at least 3 hours or as long as 3 days.

Chocolate Rum Ice Cream with Candied Chestnuts

*Candied chestnuts (*marrons glacés*) usually come in cans or jars from France or Italy. Look for them in specialty food shops or in the fancy foods section of well-stocked supermarkets. This soft and luscious ice cream will add a sophisticated air to any meal.*

Makes about 1½ quarts

---

1 (5-ounce) can candied chestnuts, finely chopped (about 1 cup)
1 recipe Chocolate Rum Ice Cream (page 19)

---

1. Spread the chopped chestnuts in a single layer in a pie plate or other shallow pan. Cover and refrigerate until needed.
2. Prepare Chocolate Rum Ice Cream through step 2. Whisk the mixture to blend and pour into the canister of an ice cream maker. Freeze according to the manufacturer's directions.
3. When the ice cream is at the soft-serve stage, add the cold chestnuts (along with the rum called for in the ice cream) and process 1 minute longer. Transfer to a covered container and freeze at least 3 hours or as long as 3 days.

White Chocolate Chip Ice Cream with Macadamia Nuts

This deceptively innocent-looking white ice cream packs a lot of unexpected flavor and crunch. In fact, I think it deserves to be scooped into crystal wine goblets, drizzled with Kahlúa, and garnished with one or two Chocolate Leaves (page 94). Alternatively, just dig into the freezer container with a big spoon.

Makes about 1¾ quarts

---

1 cup roasted whole salted or unsalted macadamia nuts (about 4 ounces), coarsely chopped
⅔ cup white chocolate chips, vanilla milk chips, or classic white chips
1 recipe White Chocolate Ice Cream (page 21)

---

1. In a medium bowl, combine the chopped nuts and chocolate chips. Cover and refrigerate until needed.
2. Prepare White Chocolate Ice Cream through step 2. Whisk the mixture to blend and pour into the canister of an ice cream maker. Freeze according to the manufacturer's directions.
3. When the ice cream is at the soft-serve stage, add the macadamia nuts and white chocolate chips and process 1 minute longer. Transfer to a covered container and freeze at least 3 hours or as long as 3 days.

Chocolate Malt Ice Cream with Malt Balls

Malt balls look their best when neatly cut in half, but if you're rushed for time simply break them into large pieces by crushing gently under a heavy pot.

Makes about 1½ quarts

---

1 (3.4-ounce) box malted milk balls, such as Whoppers (about 1 cup)
1 recipe Chocolate Malt Ice Cream (page 22)

---

1. Using a sharp knife, cut each malt ball in half. Cover and refrigerate until needed.
2. Prepare Chocolate Malt Ice Cream through step 3. Pour the custard into the canister of an ice cream maker and freeze according to the manufacturer's directions.
3. When the ice cream is at the soft-serve stage, add the cold malted milk balls and process 1 minute longer. Transfer to a covered container and freeze at least 3 hours or as long as 3 days.

Vanilla Cookie Dough Ice Cream

There are those who can't keep their hands out of the cookie jar, and those who can't keep their fingers out of the bowl of raw cookie dough. If you fall into the latter group, this one's for you. Any packaged cookie dough will do; just be sure the flavor is compatible with the ice cream you select.

Makes about 1½ quarts

½ package (about 10 ounces) refrigerated cookie dough (any flavor, such as fudge brownie or chocolate chip)
1 recipe French Vanilla Ice Cream (page 11)

---

1. Cut or pull off ¾-inch chunks of cookie dough to equal 1 to 1½ cups. Arrange the pieces in a single layer on a baking sheet or another shallow pan. Cover and freeze until needed.

2. Prepare French Vanilla Ice Cream through step 3. Pour the custard into the canister of an ice cream maker and freeze according to the manufacturer's directions.

3. When the ice cream is at the soft-serve stage, add the frozen cookie dough chunks and process 1 minute longer. Transfer to a covered container and freeze at least 3 hours or as long as 3 days.

Candy Crunch Ice Cream

Adding chunks of your favorite candy bar to ice cream delivers a new flavor and texture you and any kids in the vicinity are sure to love. Just about any candy, like Snickers, Butterfinger, Milky Way, Rolo, Kit Kat, Peanut Brittle, or whole M&Ms, can rejuvenate a jaded palate. And don't forget homemade or store-bought fudge. The procedure is always the same: chop the candy into small chunks and chill before adding.

Makes about 1½ quarts

---

1 cup coarsely chopped chocolate-covered English toffee candy, such as Heath Bars or
   Almond Roca (about 6 ounces)
1 recipe French Vanilla (page 11) or Café au Lait Ice Cream (page 25)

---

1. Place the candy pieces in a small bowl. Cover and refrigerate until needed.
2. Prepare French Vanilla Ice Cream through step 3. Pour the custard into the canister of an ice cream maker and freeze according to the manufacturer's directions.
3. When the ice cream is at the soft-serve stage, add the cold candy pieces and process 1 minute longer. Transfer to a covered container and freeze at least 3 hours or as long as 3 days.

Praline Swirl Ice Cream

Crunchy caramelized nuts make this a delightful choice for both a casual and a more sophisticated frozen treat. With a cache of Nutty Praline (page 95) tucked away in a covered container, this fancy flavor can be whipped up in a flash.

Makes about 1½ quarts.

Nutty Praline (page 95)
1 recipe Voluptuous Vanilla Ice Cream (page 14)

---

1. Place the praline in a bowl. Cover and refrigerate until cold.

2. Prepare Voluptuous Vanilla Ice Cream through step 3. Whisk the custard to blend and pour into the canister of an ice cream maker. Freeze according to the manufacturer's directions.

3. When the ice cream is at the soft-serve stage, add the cold praline and process 1 minute longer. Eat at once or transfer to a covered container and freeze up to 8 hours.

Mocha Latte 'n' Cookies Ice Cream

Cookies have been served alongside ice cream for as long as anyone can remember. So why not combine these two favorites into one fabulous new flavor? Homemade brownies or cookies, such as Coconut Mocha-Nut Macaroons (page 76), are always a special treat, but store-bought cookies work surprisingly well. Peruse the cookie aisle of your local supermarket and you're sure to come up with some great ideas. Chunks of crunchy biscotti, crème-filled chocolate sandwich cookies such as Oreos, chocolate-covered graham crackers, chocolate chip cookies, oatmeal cookies, and Mystic Mints are just some of mine.

Makes about 1½ quarts

1½ cups coarsely chopped gingersnaps
1 recipe Mocha Ice Cream (page 23) or flavor of your choice

---

1. Place the cookies in a small bowl. Cover and refrigerate until needed.
2. Prepare Mocha Ice Cream through step 2. Whisk the mixture to blend and pour into the canister of an ice cream maker. Freeze according to the manufacturer's directions.
3. When the ice cream is at the soft-serve stage, add the cold cookies and process 1 minute longer. Transfer to a covered container and freeze at least 3 hours or as long as 3 days.

Truffled Espresso Bean Ice Cream

Not the pungent mushroom, the intense chocolate candies, of course, make this a sweet but sophisticated treat. The miniature chocolate truffles can be made in advance and refrigerated up to 5 days or frozen up to 1 month. Just be sure to store them in an airtight container so they don't absorb any other aromas from your refrigerator. These truffles are also delicious to eat as is, or they can be used in Frozen Italian Fantasy (page 194).

Makes about 1¾ quarts

---

4 ounces bittersweet or semisweet chocolate, coarsely chopped
⅓ cup heavy cream
3 tablespoons unsweetened cocoa powder
1 recipe Espresso Bean Ice Cream (page 26)

---

1. Place the chocolate and cream in a small heatproof bowl. Place the bowl over a saucepan of simmering water and heat, stirring, until the chocolate is melted and the mixture is smooth and blended, 5 to 7 minutes.

2. Remove the bowl from the heat and let cool, stirring occasionally, for 30 minutes. Cover and refrigerate until firm, about 2 hours.

3. Pour the cocoa powder into a pie plate or shallow pan. Using a melon baller or a teaspoon, scrape out the chocolate mixture to form a rough ball about ½ inch in diameter. Working quickly, roll each ball between your palms until smooth, then place in the pie plate with the cocoa powder. Repeat with the remaining truffle mixture to make 15 to 20 truffles. Gently shake the pie plate to coat the truffles with cocoa. Cover and refrigerate until very cold, at least 2 hours.

4. Prepare Espresso Bean Ice Cream through step 5. Pour the custard into the canister of an ice cream maker and freeze according to the manufacturer's directions.

5. Lift the chilled truffles from the cocoa powder, shaking off any excess. Transfer the ice cream to a large freezer container. Using a rubber spatula, gently fold in about half of the truffles. Repeat with the remaining truffles. Cover and freeze at least 3 hours or as long as 3 days.

Chunky Peanut Fudge Ripple Ice Cream

If there's anything better than peanut butter, it's peanut butter ice cream enhanced with nuggets of roasted peanuts and swirls of fudgy chocolate. Additions of this delectable duo work great with other ice creams, such as French Vanilla (page 11), Brown Sugar (page 44), and White Chocolate (page 21) as well.

Makes about 1½ quarts

---

1 recipe Utterly Peanut Butter Ice Cream (page 37)
⅔ cup Hot Fudge Sauce (page 82)
½ cup salted or unsalted roasted peanuts, coarsely chopped

---

1. Prepare Utterly Peanut Butter Ice Cream through step 4. Pour the custard into the canister of an ice cream maker and freeze according to the manufacturer's directions.
2. Meanwhile, in a small saucepan, warm the Hot Fudge Sauce over low heat, stirring, until melted and smooth. Remove from the heat and let cool slightly, about 5 minutes.
3. When the ice cream is at the soft-serve stage, add the peanuts and process 1 minute longer. Pour in the Hot Fudge Sauce and process until swirled throughout, 30 to 60 seconds. Transfer to a covered container and freeze at least 3 hours or as long as 3 days.

Peanut Butter Ice Cream with Chocolate-Covered Raisins

A bowl of salted peanuts and raisins has always been a favorite party snack; now these flavors can be captured in one luscious ice cream. In fact, you will find that chocolate-covered raisins also make a great addition to Butter Pecan (page 30), Classic Chocolate (page 16), and many other ice creams.

Makes about 1½ quarts

---

1 (10-ounce) package semisweet chocolate-covered raisins (1⅓ cups)
1 recipe Utterly Peanut Butter Ice Cream (page 37)

---

1. Spread the chocolate-covered raisins in a single layer in a pie plate or other shallow pan. Cover and refrigerate until needed.
2. Prepare Utterly Peanut Butter Ice Cream through step 4. Pour the custard into the canister of an ice cream maker and freeze according to the manufacturer's directions.
3. When the ice cream is at the soft-serve stage, add the cold chocolate-covered raisins and process 1 minute longer. Transfer to a covered container and freeze at least 3 hours or as long as 3 days.

Mint Chocolate Chip Ice Cream

Makes about 1½ quarts

1 recipe Peppermint Ice Cream (page 50)
¼ teaspoon green food coloring
1 cup coarsely chopped thin chocolate mints, such as Andes

1. Prepare Peppermint Ice Cream through step 3, but omit the crushed peppermint sticks, increase the peppermint extract to 1 teaspoon, and add the green food coloring. Add the food coloring with the extracts.
2. Place the candy in a small bowl. Cover and refrigerate or freeze until needed.
3. Pour the custard into the canister of an ice cream maker and freeze according to the manufacturer's directions.
4. When the ice cream is at the soft-serve stage, add the cold candy and process 1 minute longer. Transfer to a covered container and freeze at least 3 hours or as long as 3 days.

Candied Peppermint Fudge Ripple Ice Cream

Peppermint lovers will be delighted to find a fudgy ribbon of chocolate infused with more of their favored refreshing flavor.

Makes about 1¾ quarts

---

1 recipe Peppermint Ice Cream (page 50)
1 cup Peppermint Hot Fudge Sauce (page 83)

---

1. Prepare Peppermint Ice Cream through step 3. Pour the custard into the canister of an ice cream maker and freeze according to the manufacturer's directions.

2. Meanwhile, in a small heavy saucepan, warm the Peppermint Hot Fudge Sauce over low heat, stirring, until smooth. Remove from the heat and let cool slightly, about 5 minutes.

3. When the ice cream mixture is at the soft-serve stage, pour in the Peppermint Hot Fudge Sauce and the remaining ½ cup crushed peppermint candy and process until swirled throughout, 30 seconds to 1 minute. Transfer to a covered container and freeze at least 3 hours or as long as 3 days.

Brown Sugar Ice Cream with Toasted Almonds and Amaretto

When added to ice cream, almonds seem to maintain their crunch better than other nuts. For maximum "crunch-ability," toast nuts before adding to ice cream.

Makes about 1½ quarts

---

1 cup whole almonds with skins (about 4 ounces)
1 recipe Brown Sugar Ice Cream (page 44)
3 tablespoons amaretto (almond liqueur)

---

1. Preheat the oven to 325°F. Spread out the almonds on a baking sheet and toast in the oven, shaking the pan several times, until lightly browned, 8 to 10 minutes. Let cool. Chop coarsely into ½-inch pieces.
2. Prepare Brown Sugar Ice Cream through step 2. Whisk the mixture to blend and pour into the canister of an ice cream maker. Freeze according the manufacturer's directions.
3. When the ice cream is at the soft-serve stage, add the toasted almonds and amaretto and process 1 minute longer. Transfer to a covered container and freeze at least 3 hours or as long as 3 days.

Apple Butter Swirl Maple Nut Ice Cream

For a truly memorable treat, place a generous scoop of this over a warm slice of homemade apple pie.

Makes about 1½ quarts

---

1 recipe Maple Walnut Ice Cream (page 29)
⅔ cup apple butter
2 tablespoons unsalted butter, cut into 4 pieces

---

1. Prepare Maple Walnut Ice Cream through step 2. Whisk the mixture to blend and pour the custard into the canister of an ice cream maker. Freeze according to the manufacturer's directions.

2. Meanwhile, in a small saucepan, warm the apple butter and butter over low heat, stirring, until the butter melts and the mixture is smooth. Remove from the heat and let cool slightly, about 5 minutes.

3. When the ice cream is at the soft-serve stage, add the toasted walnuts and process 1 minute longer. Pour in the apple butter mixture and process just until swirled throughout, 30 to 60 seconds. Transfer to a covered container and freeze at least 3 hours or as long as 3 days.

Pumpkin Ice Cream with
Hazelnuts and Chocolate

This distinctive flavor can be made any time of year with canned pumpkin, but it's particularly appropriate for fall entertaining. On special occasions or for holiday dinners, consider serving a scoop in a chocolate shell.

Makes about 1¾ quarts

---

1 cup hazelnuts (filberts)
4 ounces bittersweet or semisweet chocolate, well chilled
1 recipe Pumpkin Pie Ice Cream (page 48)

---

1. Preheat the oven to 325°F. Spread out the hazelnuts on a baking sheet. Toast in the oven, shaking the pan several times, until the nuts are lightly browned and fragrant and the dark skins are cracked, 10 to 12 minutes. Rub the warm nuts in a terrycloth towel to remove as much of the skin as possible.

2. Using the large holes on a hand grater, coarsely grate the cold chocolate. Place in a small bowl, cover, and refrigerate until needed.

3. Prepare Pumpkin Pie Ice Cream through step 3. Stir the pumpkin custard and pour into the canister of an ice cream maker. Freeze according to the manufacturer's directions.

4. When the ice cream is at the soft-serve stage, add the toasted hazelnuts and cold chocolate and process 1 minute longer. Transfer to a covered container and freeze at least 3 hours or as long as 3 days.

Cinnamon Fudge Ripple Ice Cream

To my way of thinking, hot fudge sauce is like a very expensive strand of pearls: it goes with everything. In this particular case, smooth rich chocolate is an elegant complement to spicy cinnamon. You see, it's all a matter of taste.

Makes about 1½ quarts

---

1 recipe Cinnamon Ice Cream (page 41)
1 cup Hot Fudge Sauce (page 82)

---

1. Prepare Cinnamon Ice Cream through step 4. Pour the custard into the canister of an ice cream maker and freeze according to the manufacturer's directions.
2. Meanwhile, in a small saucepan, warm the Hot Fudge Sauce over low heat, stirring, until smooth. Remove from the heat and let cool slightly, about 5 minutes.
3. When the ice cream is at the soft-serve stage, pour in the cooled fudge sauce and process just until swirled throughout, 30 to 60 seconds. Transfer to a covered container and freeze at least 3 hours or as long as 3 days.

Coconut Mocha-Nut Macaroon Ice Cream

This easy recipe makes more chewy little macaroons than you'll need for the ice cream, but I assure you they won't go to waste. If your family doesn't eat them up at once, they can also be used in the Crazy for Coconut Ice Cream Log (page 196). The cookies will stay fresh for several days at room temperature in an airtight container: freeze them for longer storage.

Makes about 1¾ quarts

---

1 cup whole almonds with skins (about 4 ounces)

1 (14-ounce) can sweetened condensed milk

2 (1-ounce) squares unsweetened chocolate, chopped

1½ teaspoons instant espresso powder

1 (7-ounce) package sweetened flaked or shredded coconut

1 teaspoon almond extract

⅛ teaspoon salt

1 recipe Caribbean Coconut Ice Cream (page 40)

---

1. Preheat the oven to 325°F. Spread out the almonds on a baking sheet and toast in the oven, shaking the pan several times, until lightly browned, 8 to 10 minutes. Let cool. Chop coarsely into ½-inch pieces. Increase the oven temperature to 350°F.

2. In a large heavy saucepan, combine the sweetened condensed milk, chocolate, and instant espresso powder. Cook over medium heat, stirring, until the chocolate melts and the mixture is thick and glossy, 5 to 7 minutes. Remove from the heat and stir in the almonds, coconut, almond extract, and salt.

3. Drop the mixture by tablespoons onto greased cookie sheets to make 42 to 48 cookies. Bake until the bottoms are just set, about 12 minutes; the macaroons will be soft and chewy. Transfer to wax paper to cool.

4. Cut or tear enough macaroons (about 8) into ½-inch pieces to equal 1 cup. Arrange the pieces in a single layer in a pie plate or other shallow pan. Cover and freeze until needed. Place the remaining macaroons in an airtight container and eat as cookies or reserve for other uses.

5. Prepare Caribbean Coconut Ice Cream through step 4. Pour the custard into the canister of an ice cream maker and freeze according to the manufacturer's directions. When the ice cream is at the soft-serve stage, add the frozen Coconut Mocha-Nut Macaroon pieces (along with the coconut called for in the ice cream) and process 1 minute longer. Transfer to a covered container and freeze at least 3 hours or as long as 3 days.

Pecan Butterscotch Ripple Ice Cream

This golden pairing looks most inviting served in a stemmed wineglass and topped with a sprinkling of toasted pecans. A little drizzle of Hot Fudge Sauce (page 82) would gild the lily, as it were.

Makes about 1½ quarts

---

1 recipe Butter Pecan Ice Cream (page 30)
1 cup Best Butterscotch Sauce (page 90)

---

1. Prepare Butter Pecan Ice Cream through step 4. Pour the custard into the canister of an ice cream maker and freeze according to the manufacturer's directions.
2. Meanwhile, in a small saucepan, warm the butterscotch sauce over low heat, stirring, until melted and smooth. Remove from the heat and let cool slightly, about 5 minutes.
3. When the ice cream is at the soft-serve stage, add the toasted pecans from step 1 of Butter Pecan Ice Cream and process 1 minute longer. Pour in the butterscotch sauce and process just until swirled throughout, 30 to 60 seconds. Transfer to a covered container and freeze at least 3 hours or as long as 3 days.

Eggnog Cranberry Swirl Ice Cream

Nothing says holiday better than eggnog and cranberries. This heady ice cream with its sweet-tart swirl not only has terrific eye appeal, but it also passes the taste test with flying colors.

Makes about 1½ quarts

1½ cups fresh or frozen cranberries (6 ounces)
⅓ cup sugar
½ cup light corn syrup

⅓ cup dry red wine or water
1 recipe Eggnog Ice Cream (page 49)

---

1. Pick over the cranberries to remove any stems or badly bruised fruit. In a medium nonreactive saucepan, combine the cranberries, sugar, corn syrup, and wine. Cover and cook over medium-low heat until the cranberries pop, about 10 minutes. Remove from the heat and let cool slightly.

2. In a blender or food processor, puree the cranberry mixture until smooth. Transfer to a small bowl and let cool to room temperature. Cover and refrigerate until very cold, at least 2 hours.

3. Prepare Eggnog Ice Cream through step 4 but do not remove from the canister. After processing the brandy and rum for 1 minute, add the cold cranberry puree and process until swirled throughout, 30 to 60 seconds longer. Transfer to a covered container and freeze at least 3 hours or as long as 3 days.

Lemon Blackberry Swirl Ice Cream

While lemon and blackberries form a beautiful pair, a swirl of berry puree comple-
ments a myriad of ice cream flavors, so let your imagination run wild. Experiment
by varying the type of ice cream as well as the berries, such as Vanilla Ice Cream
(page 10) with a boysenberry swirl or Peaches 'n' Cream (page 34) with raspberry.
Always taste the berry puree first, adjusting the amount of sugar according to the
sweetness of the fruit and adding a bit of fresh lemon juice when needed.

Makes about 1½ quarts

---

4 cups (2 pints) fresh blackberries or frozen unsweetened blackberries, thawed
⅔ cup sugar
1 recipe Lemon Custard Ice Cream (page 36)

---

1. In a large bowl, mash the berries into a coarse puree using a fork. Stir in the sugar.
Let stand 1 hour, stirring several times. Cover and refrigerate at least 2 hours or as long
as 1 day.
2. Prepare Lemon Custard Ice Cream through step 6. Stir the lemon custard and pour
into the canister of an ice cream maker. Freeze according the manufacturer's directions.
When the ice cream is at the soft-serve stage, add the cold blackberry puree and process
just until swirled throughout, 30 to 60 seconds. Transfer to a covered container and freeze
at least 3 hours or as long as 3 days.

Persimmon Swirl Ice Cream

I find brilliant orange persimmons so irresistible that when they first come into season I usually go a little overboard, piling them onto decorative platters and baskets throughout my house. They look stunning for a week or two, and then they suddenly ripen—losing all visual appeal, becoming bloated and mushy. This ice cream has been a longtime favorite recipe for using this ugly but delicious fruit.

Makes about 1½ quarts

---

1 cup persimmon pulp (about 4 large, very ripe Hachiya persimmons)
6 tablespoons Grand Marnier or other orange-flavored liqueur
1 recipe Vanilla Ice Cream (page 10)

---

1. In a food processor, combine the persimmon pulp and Grand Marnier. Puree until smooth. Transfer the mixture to a small bowl, cover, and refrigerate until needed.
2. Prepare Vanilla Ice Cream through step 2. Whisk the mixture to blend and pour into the canister of an ice cream maker. Freeze according to the manufacturer's directions. When the mixture is at the soft-serve stage, add the persimmon mixture and process until swirled throughout, 1 to 2 minutes longer. Eat at once or transfer to a covered container and freeze up to 8 hours.

Hot Fudge Sauce

This sauce pours on hot and silky, transforming into chewy fudge as it cools. It can be prepared a week in advance and stored, covered, in the refrigerator; warm over low heat before serving.

Makes about 2 cups

¾ cup sugar
1 stick (4 ounces) unsalted butter, cut into tablespoons
½ cup heavy cream
¼ cup light corn syrup
Dash of salt

4 ounces bittersweet or semisweet chocolate, finely chopped
4 (1-ounce) squares unsweetened chocolate, finely chopped
2 teaspoons vanilla extract

1. In a heavy medium saucepan, combine the sugar, butter, cream, corn syrup, and salt. Cook over medium-low heat, stirring, until the sugar is dissolved and the mixture is smooth, about 5 minutes. Remove from the heat.
2. Add the chocolates and stir until melted and smooth. Stir in the vanilla.

Peppermint Hot Fudge Sauce

Add ¼ teaspoon peppermint extract with the vanilla. Taste for flavoring. Add more peppermint extract, if needed, a few drops at a time.

Hot Brandied Fudge Sauce

Add 2 tablespoons brandy with the vanilla.

Hot Fudge à l'Orange

Add 2 tablespoons minced orange zest and/or 2 tablespoons orange liqueur, such as Grand Marnier, with the vanilla.

Bittersweet Fudge Sauce

Unsweetened cocoa powder delivers deep chocolate flavor without the bother of chopping chocolate. You'll definitely want to add this one to your repertoire.

Makes about 2 cups

---

1 cup heavy cream
¾ cup sugar
4 tablespoons (½ stick) unsalted butter,
  cut into pieces

Dash of salt
¾ cup unsweetened Dutch-process cocoa
  powder

---

1. In a heavy medium saucepan, combine the cream, sugar, butter, and salt. Bring to a boil over medium heat, stirring to dissolve the sugar.
2. Reduce the heat to low and cook until thickened but not browned, about 3 minutes. Remove from the heat and whisk in the cocoa powder until smooth. Use at once or let cool completely. Cover and refrigerate up to 1 week and warm over low heat before serving.

Rich Chocolate Sauce

This classic French ganache *makes an easy and luscious sauce for ice cream. If made in advance, cover and refrigerate up to one week and warm over low heat before serving.*

Makes about 1½ cups

---

1 cup heavy cream
Dash of salt
8 ounces bittersweet or semisweet chocolate, finely chopped

---

1. In a small heavy saucepan, combine the cream and salt. Bring to a boil over medium heat.
2. Remove from the heat and add the chocolate, stirring until smooth. Let cool until the desired consistency is reached. (The sauce thickens as it cools.)

Easy Chocolate Sauce

Whether served warm or at room temperature, this sauce will not harden over cold ice cream.

Makes about 1¾ cups

1 cup half-and-half or light cream
1 cup sugar
2 tablespoons light corn syrup
Dash of salt

4 (1-ounce) squares unsweetened chocolate, finely chopped
2 tablespoons unsalted butter
1 teaspoon vanilla extract

1. In a heavy small saucepan, combine the half-and-half, sugar, corn syrup, and salt. Cook over medium heat, stirring, until the mixture is hot and the sugar dissolves, 3 to 5 minutes.

2. Remove from the heat. Add the chocolate and butter, stirring until melted and smooth. Stir in the vanilla. If made in advance, cover and refrigerate up to 1 week. If the sauce becomes too thick, thin it with a bit of milk, coffee, liquor, or water to reach the desired consistency.

VARIATIONS:

Chocolate Rum Sauce

Add 2 tablespoons dark rum with the vanilla.

Chocolate Ginger Sauce

Add 2 to 3 tablespoons minced crystallized ginger with the vanilla.

Chocolate Mint Sauce

Add ¼ teaspoon peppermint extract with the vanilla. Taste for flavoring. Add more peppermint extract if needed, a few drops at a time.

Homemade Chocolate Syrup

This is reminiscent of the commercial brand of syrup you grew up on—only better. The thin but flavorful sauce can be drizzled over ice cream, or used to make chocolate milk or real hot chocolate.

Makes about 1¾ cups

---

1 cup sugar
½ cup unsweetened cocoa powder,
   preferably Dutch-process

⅛ teaspoon salt
1 cup water
1 teaspoon vanilla extract

---

1. In a heavy medium saucepan, combine the sugar, cocoa powder, and salt. Gradually whisk in the water until smooth.

2. Bring to a boil over medium heat, stirring, to dissolve the sugar. Continue cooking 3 minutes longer, stirring constantly. Remove from the heat and let cool. Stir in the vanilla. If made in advance, cover and refrigerate up to 1 week.

Hot Cocoa Mocha Sauce

Serve this deep, dark sauce while it is still warm. If made in advance, store in the refrigerator, covered, up to 1 week.

Makes about 1¾ cups

---

1 cup strongly brewed coffee
¾ cup sugar
Dash of salt
¾ cup unsweetened cocoa powder, preferably Dutch-process
2 tablespoons unsalted butter, cut into 8 pieces

---

1. In a medium nonreactive saucepan, combine the coffee, sugar, and salt. Bring to a boil over medium heat, stirring to dissolve the sugar. Reduce the heat to low and whisk in the cocoa powder until smooth. Simmer 3 minutes.

2. Add the butter, stirring until melted. Simmer 3 minutes longer. Use at once or let cool and refrigerate, covered.

Best Butterscotch Sauce

This is the chocolate-free equivalent of Hot Fudge Sauce: rich, complex, and tantalizing. A golden dollop is a natural on vanilla ice cream, but try it also with flavors like Chocolate Rum (page 19) and Café au Lait (page 25).

Makes about 1⅓ cups

---

1 cup (packed) light brown sugar
½ cup heavy cream
4 tablespoons (½ stick) unsalted butter, cut into pieces
¼ cup light corn syrup

Dash of salt
1½ teaspoons vanilla extract
¼ teaspoon fresh lemon juice or cider vinegar

---

1. In a heavy small saucepan, combine the brown sugar, cream, butter, corn syrup, and salt. Bring to a boil over medium heat, stirring, until the sugar is dissolved and the butter is melted. Reduce the heat to low and simmer, without stirring, for 5 minutes.

2. Remove from the heat and let cool 5 minutes. Add the vanilla and lemon juice, stirring until smooth. Serve at once or let cool completely. Cover and refrigerate up to 1 week; warm over low heat before serving.

Double-Scotch Whiskey Sauce

Add 2 tablespoons Scotch whiskey with the vanilla and lemon juice.

Butterscotch Pecan Sauce

Add ½ cup chopped toasted pecans with the vanilla and lemon juice.

Easy Caramel Sauce

Sweetened condensed milk is a precooked blend of whole milk and sugar. When you think of it that way, it's not so surprising that long cooking results in a sauce with buttery, rich flavor.

Makes about ²/₃ cup

---

1 (14-ounce) can sweetened condensed milk

---

1. Preheat the oven to 425°F. Pour the sweetened condensed milk into a 9-inch heatproof glass pie plate and cover with aluminum foil. Place in a shallow roasting pan and fill with enough hot tap water to reach two-thirds up the sides of the pie plate.

2. Bake until the milk is thickened and caramel-colored, 1 to 1½ hours. Carefully lift the pie plate from the water bath, remove the foil, and let cool on a wire rack. Serve warm or at room temperature. If made in advance, cover and refrigerate up to 1 week. Warm over low heat before serving.

Chocolate Curls and Twirls

Once you learn to recognize the chocolate temperature needed to master these little "twirls," you'll probably want to scatter them over every dish of ice cream you serve. And why shouldn't you? In the words of Mae West, "Too much of a good thing can be wonderful."

Makes enough to garnish 4 to 6 servings

---

1 large bar or piece (4 ounces or more) bittersweet, semisweet, or imported white chocolate, at warm room temperature

---

1. Use a paper towel to hold the chocolate on edge so the heat from your fingers doesn't melt it. Working over a baking sheet lined with wax paper, use a swivel-bladed vegetable peeler to gently press against the edges of the chocolate bar and "peel" away curls. Let the curls drop onto the wax paper.
2. Refrigerate or freeze the baking sheet until the chocolate curls are firm; then cover and refrigerate or freeze until needed. To serve, use a metal spatula to lift the cold chocolate curls from the wax paper and place them on the ice cream.

TIPS:

- One ounce of chocolate will make plenty of curls for 4 to 6 servings. However, it is easier to work from a larger piece of chocolate.
- The chocolate must be slightly warm. If it is too cool, you will make splinters and shavings. If it is too warm, you will make soft, lifeless strips.
- The harder you press, the thicker the curls will be.
- Longer strokes (against the long edge of the chocolate) make more elaborate curls.
- Avoid touching the chocolate, as the heat from your fingers could be enough to melt the curls.

Chocolate Leaves

If there's a lemon tree on your block, you're halfway to making the beautiful edible chocolate leaves you've seen at bakeries. Take your time making them and don't fret if a few break in the process. (Just pop 'em in your mouth to destroy the evidence.) These can be made well in advance, so that at a moment's notice even the homeliest little scoop of ice cream can bloom into an elegant dessert.

Makes about 20

---

20 firm, nontoxic leaves (such as lemon, orange, ivy, or camellia) with ¼ to ½ inch
of stem attached
4 ounces bittersweet, semisweet, or imported white chocolate, finely chopped

---

1. Rinse the leaves with cold water and dry thoroughly. Carefully melt the chocolate in the top of a double boiler over very low heat until smooth. Let the chocolate cool until slightly thickened, 5 to 10 minutes.

2. Using a narrow metal spatula or a dull knife, spread a thick layer of chocolate on the underside of each leaf to within ¹⁄₁₆ inch of its edge. (Do not let the chocolate drip over the edges of the leaves, as it may break while peeling.) Place the leaves, chocolate-side up, on a wax paper-lined baking sheet. Refrigerate until the chocolate is firm, at least 25 minutes.

3. To remove the chocolate from the leaf, grasp the stem and gently peel the leaf away from the chocolate. Touch the chocolate as little as possible to avoid fingerprints and smudging. Refrigerate or freeze the baking sheet until the chocolate is firm; then cover and refrigerate until needed.

Nutty Praline

Praline is a brittle candy made from caramelized sugar. It can be either pulverized into a powder or broken into pieces to eat as is, use as an ingredient in ice cream and desserts, or sprinkle on top as a garnish.

Makes about 1 cup

---

1 cup nuts, such as chopped pecans, blanched slivered almonds, skinned hazelnuts, walnuts, pistachios, or pine nuts
2 teaspoons vegetable oil
½ cup sugar
1 tablespoon water

---

1. Preheat the oven to 325°F. Spread the nuts on a baking sheet and toast in the oven, shaking the pan several times, until lightly browned, 5 to 8 minutes. Let cool.
2. Line an 8-inch pan or baking sheet with aluminum foil and brush lightly with the vegetable oil.
3. In a heavy medium saucepan, combine the sugar and water. Cook over medium-low heat, stirring with a wooden spoon, until the sugar has melted and the syrup is golden. (Test by dropping a little on a white plate.) Add the nuts and cook, stirring until the nuts are well coated and the syrup is amber, about 30 seconds longer.
4. Scrape the mixture onto aluminum foil and spread in a thin layer. Let cool completely. When the praline is hard, break or chop into ¼-inch pieces. (The praline can be made a week in advance and stored airtight at room temperature.) Before making the ice cream, put the praline in a bowl, cover, and refrigerate until needed.

Caramel Icicles

Most upscale restaurants now serve some sort of contrived "architectural" dessert that is both fascinating to look at and impossible to eat. But a golden shard of crunchy caramel jutting out of a serving of homemade ice cream is another matter altogether. Now this is a garnish that makes sense (and tastes great).

Makes enough to garnish about 12 desserts

¼ cup water
½ cup sugar

---

1. Line a baking sheet with parchment paper or foil and brush lightly with vegetable oil. In a small saucepan, mix the water with the sugar until moistened. Cover and bring to a simmer over medium heat. Without stirring, wipe down the sides of the pan with a damp pastry brush or paper towel to remove any sugar crystals. Cover and cook until the sugar is dissolved, about 2 minutes longer. Uncover and cook without stirring until the sugar is golden. (Test by dropping a little on a white plate.) Swirl the pan gently, continuing to test the color, until the syrup is amber.
2. Immediately pour the caramel onto the prepared baking sheet, carefully tilting the sheet to spread the caramel as thinly as possible. Let cool completely.
3. Carefully peel the parchment away from the caramel, breaking off jagged, irregularly shaped pieces of caramel as you go. The Caramel Icicles can be stored between layers of parchment or wax paper in an airtight container at room temperature for 2 days.

Chapter Three
On the Lighter Side

No matter how rich and filling dinner may be, most of us crave just a little something sweet to finish it off. This chapter features a dazzling array of flavorful ice creams made without eggs or heavy cream and frozen fat-free yogurts that allow you to enjoy dessert and lighten things up at the same time.

Don't confuse these ethereal concoctions with the bland commercial "ice milks" of yesteryear, for the flavors here are lively and true, mellowed with a minimum of sweetening. Some, like Pear-Ginger Light Ice Cream, are made with half-and-half for a touch of richness without all the fat. Others, like Tangy Orange Iced Buttermilk, rely on low-fat buttermilk for their creaminess. And don't miss the unexpected satin derived from fat-free sweetened condensed milk in Enlightened Frozen Eggnog.

A mug of Frozen Hot Cocoa is welcome anytime of year. And a spot of Earl Grey Tea Light Ice Cream is just the thing to end the day. Creamy Banana Light Ice Cream, laden with ripe fruit puree, is also sure to make a repeat performance in your kitchen. Richer than sorbets, these light ice creams are reminiscent of American-style sherbets, but there's nothing old-fashioned about them—they're simply in a class by themselves.

When frozen yogurt hit the market a decade or so ago, it was a dream come true for those of us who like to indulge frequently. We could delight in the deep, rich flavor and never have to worry about the missing fat. Armed with little more than your trusty ice cream maker, you can now create your own low-fat or nonfat favorites, using only the finest ingredients. You and your guests will revel in the luscious quality of frozen yogurts with names like Blast-of-Chocolate, Honey Vanilla, and Red Raspberry. Who cares if they may actually be good for you?

Due to their delicate nature—and the lack of butterfat and sugar to stabilize them—light ice creams and frozen yogurts are at their best when eaten the same day they are made. They will freeze into an icy-textured mass, but soften to their original glory after 5 or 10 minutes at room temperature.

This chapter closes with light and satisfying low-fat and fat-free sauces, ideal for slathering on just about any ice cream, sorbet, or frozen dessert. You need not be a weight watcher to find your thrill with Blueberry Cinnamon Sauce and indulge in the low-fat ecstasy of Chocolate Fluff. These guilt-free recipes can easily be incorporated into any ice cream lover's repertoire.

Enlightened Vanilla Ice Cream

Makes about 1 quart

---

3 cups half-and-half or light cream
½ cup sugar, or more to taste
2 teaspoons vanilla extract

---

1. In a large bowl, combine the half-and-half, ½ cup sugar, and vanilla, whisking to blend. Taste and add more sugar if needed. Refrigerate until very cold, at least 3 hours or as long as 3 days.

2. Whisk the mixture to blend and pour into the canister of an ice cream maker. Freeze according to the manufacturer's directions. Eat at once or transfer to a covered container and freeze up to 4 hours.

VARIATIONS:

Vanilla-Caramel Swirl Ice Cream

Make Easy Caramel Sauce (page 92) using fat-free sweetened condensed milk. When the ice cream is at the soft-serve stage, add the chilled caramel sauce and process just until swirled throughout, about 1 minute longer.

Brandied Vanilla-Apricot Swirl Ice Cream

Combine 1 (10-ounce) jar no-sugar-added apricot spreadable fruit or jam with 2 tablespoons brandy; whisk to blend. Cover and refrigerate until needed. When the ice cream is at the soft-serve stage, add the apricot mixture and process just until swirled throughout, about 1 minute longer.

Choco-Light Ice Cream

If you don't have Homemade Chocolate Syrup on hand, the store-bought variety will work fine. For a double dose of flavor you may want to drizzle a bit more syrup over each serving.

Makes about 1 quart

---

3 cups half-and-half or light cream
½ cup Homemade Chocolate Syrup (page 88)
¼ cup sugar, or more to taste

½ teaspoon vanilla extract
Dash of salt

---

1. In a large bowl, combine the half-and-half, chocolate syrup, ¼ cup sugar, and vanilla, whisking to blend well. Taste and add more sugar if needed. Cover and refrigerate until very cold, at least 3 hours or as long as 3 days.

2. Whisk the mixture briefly to blend and pour into the canister of an ice cream maker. Freeze according to the manufacturer's directions. Eat at once or transfer to a covered container and freeze up to 4 hours.

Choco-Light Chip Ice Cream

When the ice cream is at the soft-serve stage, add ¾ cup chilled semisweet chocolate mini morsels or chocolate chips and process 1 minute longer.

Choco-Light Mint Ice Cream

Add ½ teaspoon peppermint extract to the base along with the vanilla.

Frozen Hot Cocoa

Behold, the steaming-hot beverage that comforted us through childhood takes on an icy new identity! Serve this in frosty little mugs or goblets, garnished with a twist of orange peel or a fresh mint sprig.

Makes about 1 quart

½ cup unsweetened cocoa powder, preferably Dutch-process
¾ cup sugar
⅛ teaspoon salt

3 cups half-and-half or light cream
1 teaspoon vanilla extract

---

1. In a nonreactive medium saucepan, combine the cocoa powder, sugar, and salt. Add ½ cup of the half-and-half and whisk until smooth. Whisk in the remaining 2½ cups half-and-half.

2. Cook over medium-low heat, stirring occasionally, until the sugar dissolves and the mixture is smooth, about 5 minutes. Remove from the heat and let cool. Stir in the vanilla. Cover and refrigerate until very cold, at least 3 hours or as long as 3 days.

3. Stir the mixture to blend and pour into the canister of an ice cream maker. Freeze according to the manufacturer's directions. Eat at once or transfer to a covered container and freeze up to 4 hours.

Spirited Frozen Hot Cocoa

When the ice cream is at the soft-serve stage, add 2 tablespoons brandy; rum; orange-chocolate liqueur, such as Sabra; or chocolate-mint liqueur, such as Vandermint. Process 1 minute longer.

Creamy Banana Light Ice Cream

When I have more overripe bananas than I can use at one time, I toss the extras (whole) into the freezer. The skins turn black, but the mushy fruit inside remains ready for future ice cream making and baking. Just let the bananas thaw briefly and remove the skins.

Makes about 5 cups

---

2 cups half-and-half or light cream

1 (14-ounce) can fat-free sweetened condensed milk

½ teaspoon vanilla extract

2 overripe medium bananas

2 tablespoons fresh lemon juice

---

1. In a large bowl, combine the half-and-half, condensed milk, and vanilla. Whisk to blend. Cover and refrigerate until very cold, at least 3 hours or as long as 3 days.

2. In a small bowl, mash the bananas with the lemon juice to form a coarse puree; there will be about 1 cup. Cover and refrigerate until needed.

3. Whisk the half-and-half mixture to blend and pour into the canister of an ice cream maker. Freeze according to the manufacturer's directions. When the ice cream is at the soft-serve stage, add the mashed bananas and process 2 minutes longer. Eat at once or transfer to a covered container and freeze up to 4 hours.

VARIATIONS:

Banana Rum Light Ice Cream

Add 2 tablespoons dark (80 proof) rum along with the bananas.

Banana Nut Light Ice Cream

Add ¾ cup toasted chopped walnuts along with the bananas.

Cappuccino Light Ice Cream

This ice cream is as refreshing as a frosty glass of iced coffee, with the subtle hint of ground cinnamon for added dimension.

Makes about 1 quart

---

2 tablespoons instant espresso powder
¼ cup boiling water
3 cups half-and-half or light cream
⅔ cup sugar

1½ teaspoons vanilla extract
½ teaspoon ground cinnamon

---

1. In a large bowl, dissolve the espresso powder in the boiling water. Let cool.

2. Add the half-and-half, sugar, vanilla, and cinnamon to the espresso. Whisk to blend. Refrigerate until very cold, at least 3 hours or as long as 3 days.

3. Whisk the mixture to blend and pour into the canister of an ice cream maker. Freeze according to the manufacturer's directions. Eat at once or transfer to a covered container and freeze up to 4 hours.

VARIATION:

Brandied Cappuccino Ice Cream

When the ice cream is at the soft-serve stage, add 2 tablespoons brandy and process 1 minute longer.

Date-Rum Light Ice Cream

Orange zest and rum accent the rich flavor of dates, making this complex ice cream a real winner.

Makes about 1 quart

¾ cup finely chopped pitted dates
  (about 4 ounces)
2 tablespoons dark rum
3 cups half-and-half or light cream

½ cup (packed) light brown sugar
2 teaspoons grated orange zest
1 teaspoon vanilla extract

---

1. Place the chopped dates in a small bowl. Sprinkle the rum over the dates. Cover and refrigerate until needed.

2. In a large bowl, combine the half-and-half, brown sugar, orange zest, and vanilla. Whisk to blend. Cover and refrigerate until very cold, at least 3 hours or as long as 3 days.

3. Whisk the mixture to blend and pour into the canister of an ice cream maker. Freeze according to the manufacturer's directions. When the ice cream is at the soft-serve stage, add the chilled dates and rum and process 2 minutes longer. Eat at once or transfer to a covered container and freeze up to 4 hours.

Maple Crunch Light Ice Cream

Bits of crunchy breakfast cereal marry with pure maple flavor to make a rich-tasting ice cream.

Makes about 1 quart

---

3 cups half-and-half or light cream
½ cup pure maple syrup
2 teaspoons vanilla extract
¾ cup crunchy cereal, such as granola, bran nuggets, or crisped rice

---

1. In a large bowl, combine the half-and-half, maple syrup, and vanilla. Whisk to blend. Refrigerate until very cold, at least 3 hours or as long as 3 days.
2. Whisk the mixture to blend and pour into the canister of an ice cream maker. Freeze according to the manufacturer's directions. When the ice cream is at the soft-serve stage, add the cereal and process 1 minute longer. Eat at once or transfer to a covered container and freeze up to 4 hours.

Pear-Ginger Light Ice Cream

Of all the fruits, pears seem hardest to catch just at their peak of ripeness and taste. Consequently, I turned to always perfect canned pears to make this great flavor. Fresh ginger adds a delightful, unexpected kick.

Makes about 1 quart

---

2 (16-ounce) cans sliced Bartlett pears in heavy syrup, drained, or 3 cups peeled and sliced ripe pears (6 to 8 fresh pears)

¾ cup sugar
1 tablespoon fresh lemon juice
1¼ teaspoons grated fresh ginger
2 cups half-and-half or light cream

---

1. In a food processor or blender, combine the pears, sugar, lemon juice, and ginger. Puree until smooth.

2. Pour the pear mixture into a large bowl. Add the half-and-half and whisk to blend. Cover and refrigerate until very cold, at least 3 hours or as long as 3 days.

3. Whisk the mixture to blend and pour into the canister of an ice cream maker. Freeze according to the manufacturer's directions. Eat at once or transfer to a covered container and freeze up to 4 hours.

Boysenberry Light Ice Cream

If you happen to nod off one June day and miss the brief season for fresh boysenberries, head to the freezer case of your local supermarket for a taste of this thoroughly delectable fruit. Blackberries or raspberries also make a great light ice cream. Just adjust the sugar by tablespoons to fit the fruit.

Makes about 1 quart

---

3 cups fresh boysenberries (1½ pints) or frozen unsweetened boysenberries
⅔ cup sugar, or more to taste
1 teaspoon fresh lemon juice, or more to taste
2 cups half-and-half or light cream

---

1. If using fresh berries, rinse gently and drain in a colander. Pick over to remove any badly bruised or moldy fruit.
2. In a food processor or blender, combine the boysenberries, ⅔ cup sugar, and 1 teaspoon lemon juice. Puree until smooth.
3. Strain the berry mixture into a large bowl, pressing through as much of the juice and fruit as you can. Add the half-and-half and whisk to blend. Taste, adding more sugar or lemon juice if needed. Cover and refrigerate until very cold, at least 3 hours or as long as 3 days.
4. Whisk the mixture to blend and pour into the canister of an ice cream maker. Freeze according to the manufacturer's directions. Eat at once or transfer to a covered container and freeze up to 4 hours.

Cherry Vanilla Light Ice Cream

Bits of sweet cherries and their juice put vanilla ice cream "in the pink." Adults may wish to intensify the cherry flavor by substituting kirsch for the fresh lemon juice.

Makes about 5 cups

½ pound fresh sweet cherries or 1 cup frozen unsweetened Bing cherries, thawed

1 tablespoon sugar

1 tablespoon kirsch or fresh lemon juice

2 cups half-and-half or light cream

1 (14-ounce) can fat-free sweetened condensed milk

1 teaspoon vanilla extract

---

1. If using fresh cherries, remove any stems. Rinse well and pat dry with paper towels. Working over the bowl of a food processor to catch the juices, cut the cherries in half with a small stainless steel knife. Cut out the pit with the tip of a knife and drop the cherries into the bowl. If using thawed frozen cherries, place in the food processor.

2. Add the sugar and lemon juice to the cherries and chop coarsely. Pour into a small bowl, cover, and refrigerate until needed.

3. In a large bowl, combine the half-and-half, condensed milk, and vanilla. Whisk to blend. Cover and refrigerate until very cold, at least 3 hours or as long as 3 days.

4. Whisk the half-and-half mixture to blend and pour into the canister of an ice cream maker. Freeze according to the manufacturer's directions.

5. When the ice cream is at the soft-serve stage, add the chopped sweetened cherries and process 2 minutes longer. Eat at once or transfer to a covered container and freeze up to 4 hours.

Mango-Lime Light Ice Cream

Many supermarkets now carry refrigerated jars of sliced mango and papaya in their produce sections, making recipes like this a "tropical breeze" to fashion.

Makes about 5 cups

---

3 ripe mangoes (about 12 ounces each) or half of 1 (26-ounce) jar mango slices in
    light syrup, drained
2 cups half-and-half or light cream
⅔ cup sugar, or more to taste
Grated zest and juice of 1 lime

---

1. If using fresh mangoes, peel and cut the fruit away from the pits. In a food processor, puree the mango until smooth.
2. In a large bowl, combine the mango puree, half-and-half, ⅔ cup sugar, lime zest, and lime juice. Whisk to blend. Taste and add more sugar if needed. Cover and refrigerate until very cold, at least 3 hours or as long as 3 days.
3. Whisk the mango mixture to blend and pour into the canister of an ice cream maker. Freeze according to the manufacturer's directions. Eat at once or transfer to a covered container and freeze up to 4 hours.

Mellow Melon Light Ice Cream

For the ultimate in juicy sweetness, it pays to seek out vine-ripened melons from either a farmers' market or a reliable produce merchant. I've recommended cantaloupe in this recipe because the flesh usually has the best color, but any flavorful melon will do.

Makes about 5 cups

---

1 very ripe medium-size cantaloupe or honeydew melon
2 cups half-and-half or light cream
⅔ cup sugar, or more to taste
2 teaspoons fresh lemon or lime juice

---

1. Peel and seed the cantaloupe. Cut into 1-inch chunks and place in a food processor or blender. Puree until smooth. There will be about 2 cups puree.
2. In a large bowl, combine the cantaloupe puree, half-and-half, ⅔ cup sugar, and lemon juice. Whisk to blend. Taste and add more sugar if needed. Cover and refrigerate until very cold, at least 3 hours or as long as 3 days.
3. Whisk the melon mixture to blend and pour into the canister of an ice cream maker. Freeze according to the manufacturer's directions. Eat at once or transfer to a covered container and freeze up to 4 hours.

Enlightened Frozen Eggnog

Eggnog without eggs? Why not? The "cooked" flavor of condensed milk gives the added illusion of richness.

Makes about 1 quart

---

2 cups half-and-half or light cream
1 (14-ounce) can fat-free sweetened condensed milk
2 teaspoons vanilla extract

1 teaspoon freshly grated nutmeg or
  ½ teaspoon ground nutmeg
2 tablespoons brandy or rum

---

1. In a large bowl, combine the half-and-half, condensed milk, vanilla, and nutmeg. Whisk to blend. Cover and refrigerate until very cold, at least 3 hours or as long as 3 days.
2. Whisk the mixture to blend and pour into the canister of an ice cream maker. Freeze according to the manufacturer's directions.
3. When the ice cream is at the soft-serve stage, add the brandy and process 1 minute longer. Eat at once or transfer to a covered container and freeze up to 4 hours.

Earl Grey Tea Light Ice Cream

Many Asian restaurants now feature East-meets-West desserts, often flavored with tea or ginger. For best taste, use full-flavored, strong black tea. Flavored teas, such as black currant or peppermint, also make good ice cream.

Makes about 1 quart

---

1 cup boiling water

2 tablespoons black tea leaves, such as
    Earl Grey

½ cup honey, or more to taste

2 cups half-and-half or light cream

1 tablespoon orange or lemon juice

---

1. In a medium heatproof bowl, pour the boiling water over the tea leaves and let steep 5 minutes. Strain through a fine sieve to remove all bits of tea leaves and let cool.

2. In a large bowl, combine the cooled tea with ½ cup honey. Whisk to blend. Whisk in the half-and-half and orange juice. Taste and add more honey if needed. Cover and refrigerate until very cold, at least 3 hours or as long as 3 days.

3. Whisk the mixture to blend and pour into the canister of an ice cream maker. Freeze according to the manufacturer's directions. Eat at once or transfer to a covered container and freeze up to 4 hours.

Tangy Orange Iced Buttermilk

This delicate ice cream has a subtle orange flavor and pleasantly icy texture that literally melts in your mouth. If you feel the need for a chocolate fix, drizzle with Homemade Chocolate Syrup (page 88).

Makes about 1 quart

---

2 medium oranges
2 cups buttermilk
¾ cup sugar

---

1. Using a vegetable brush and warm water, wash the oranges well to remove any pesticides or wax. Pat dry.

2. Using a swivel-bladed vegetable peeler, remove only the zest—the orange part of the skin, not the bitter white pith. Chop finely; there will be about 1 tablespoon.

3. Squeeze ⅔ cup juice from the oranges. Strain to remove any seeds.

4. In a large bowl, combine the orange zest, orange juice, and buttermilk. Add the sugar and whisk to blend. Cover and refrigerate until very cold, at least 3 hours or as long as 3 days.

5. Whisk the mixture to blend and pour into the canister of an ice cream maker. Freeze according to the manufacturer's directions. Eat at once or transfer to a covered container and freeze up to 4 hours.

Honey Peach Iced Buttermilk

Golden rich honey makes a most compatible pairing with peaches and buttermilk. In fact, this tastes so good you may just forget it's a "light" ice cream.

Makes about 1 quart

---

3 cups frozen unsweetened peach slices, thawed, or 4 medium peaches (about 1½ pounds), peeled and pitted
2 tablespoons fresh lemon juice

¼ teaspoon ground cinnamon
⅓ cup honey, or more to taste
2 cups buttermilk

---

1. In a food processor or blender, combine the peaches, lemon juice, and cinnamon. Puree until smooth.

2. Pour the peach puree into a large bowl. Whisk in ⅓ cup honey and buttermilk. Taste and add more honey if needed. Cover and refrigerate until very cold, at least 3 hours or as long as 3 days.

3. Whisk the peach mixture to blend and pour into the canister of an ice cream maker. Freeze according to the manufacturer's directions. Eat at once or transfer to a covered container and freeze up to 4 hours.

Slimming Strawberry Frozen Buttermilk

Buttermilk gives the illusion of richness without added fat. It is the perfect complement to tangy strawberries.

Makes about 1 quart

---

4 cups (2 pints) very ripe fresh strawberries or frozen unsweetened strawberries
¾ cup sugar
1 teaspoon fresh lemon juice
2 cups buttermilk

---

1. In a food processor or blender, combine the strawberries, sugar, and lemon juice. Puree until smooth.
2. In a large bowl, whisk together the strawberry puree and the buttermilk until well blended. Cover and refrigerate until very cold, at least 3 hours or as long as 3 days.
3. Whisk the strawberry mixture to blend and pour into the canister of an ice cream maker. Freeze according to the manufacturer's directions. Eat at once or transfer to a covered container and freeze up to 4 hours.

Easiest Lemon Frozen Yogurt

I like my frozen lemon yogurt tart and tangy. If you demand a bit less "pucker power," add a few more tablespoons of sugar. This is one of the rare recipes where I begin with a commercially flavored yogurt.

Makes about 1 quart

---

3 cups lemon-flavored low-fat or nonfat yogurt
½ cup sugar, or more to taste
Grated zest of 2 lemons

---

1. In a medium bowl, stir together the yogurt, ½ cup sugar, and the lemon zest until the sugar dissolves and the mixture is well blended, about 2 minutes. Taste and stir in more sugar if needed. Cover and refrigerate until very cold, at least 3 hours or as long as 3 days.

2. Scrape the yogurt into the canister of an ice cream maker and freeze according to the manufacturer's directions. Eat at once or transfer to a covered container and freeze up to 4 hours.

Red Raspberry Frozen Yogurt

This intensely flavored yogurt bears little resemblance to the anemic pink stuff you buy in little cartons. If your local farmers' market features less common berry varieties, such as golden or black raspberries, try them for fun as well as for flavor.

Makes about 1½ pints

4 cups (2 pints) fresh raspberries or frozen unsweetened raspberries
¾ cup sugar, or more to taste
2 cups plain low-fat or nonfat yogurt

1. If using fresh berries, rinse gently and drain in a colander. Pick over to remove any badly bruised or moldy fruit.
2. In a food processor or blender, combine the raspberries and ¾ cup sugar. Puree until smooth.
3. Strain the berry mixture into a large bowl to remove the seeds; press through as much of the juice and fruit as you can. Add the yogurt and whisk to blend. Taste and add more sugar if needed. Cover and refrigerate until very cold, at least 3 hours or as long as 3 days.
4. Scrape the yogurt into the canister of an ice cream maker and freeze according to the manufacturer's directions. Eat at once or transfer to a covered container and freeze up to 4 hours.

Strawberry Banana Frozen Yogurt

When yogurt producers first combined two of America's favorite fruits into one yummy flavor, sales skyrocketed. It's still a great idea, and homemade is an even better one.

Makes about 1 quart

---

2 cups (1 pint) fresh strawberries, rinsed and hulled, or frozen unsweetened strawberries, thawed
2 overripe medium bananas, cut into 1-inch pieces

½ cup sugar, or more to taste
2 cups plain low-fat or nonfat yogurt
2 teaspoons vanilla extract

---

1. In a food processor or blender, combine the strawberries, bananas, and ½ cup sugar. Puree until smooth. Add the yogurt and vanilla and process until well blended. Taste and add more sugar if needed.

2. Transfer the mixture to a medium bowl. Cover and refrigerate until very cold, at least 3 hours or as long as 3 days.

3. Scrape the yogurt into the canister of an ice cream maker and freeze according to the manufacturer's directions. Eat at once or transfer to a covered container and freeze up to 4 hours.

Honey Vanilla Frozen Yogurt

Rich, golden honey and fragrant, pure vanilla give this simple-sounding dessert four-star quality. Use as a topping for fruit or other desserts, or eat as is, perhaps drizzled with a bit of Spiced Honey-Bourbon Sauce (page 124).

Makes about 5 cups

---

1 quart plain low-fat or nonfat yogurt
⅓ cup honey, or more to taste
1 tablespoon vanilla extract

---

1. In a medium bowl, whisk together the yogurt, ⅓ cup honey, and vanilla to blend well. Taste and whisk in more honey if needed. Cover and refrigerate until very cold, at least 3 hours or as long as 3 days.
2. Scrape the yogurt into the canister of an ice cream maker and freeze according to the manufacturer's directions. Eat at once or transfer to a covered container and freeze up to 4 hours.

VARIATION:

Honey Vanilla Apricot Frozen Yogurt

Place ½ cup finely chopped dried apricots in a heatproof bowl and add hot water to cover. Let stand 15 minutes. Drain well. Cover and refrigerate until needed. When the frozen yogurt is at the soft-serve stage, add the apricots and process 1 minute longer.

Blast-of-Chocolate Frozen Yogurt

It's hard to believe anything that tastes this wickedly good is actually low in fat. Cocoa powder carries deep chocolaty flavor with hardly any of the cocoa fat that goes into the solid candy.

Makes about 5 cups

---

1 quart plain low-fat or nonfat yogurt
1 cup sugar, or more to taste
½ cup unsweetened cocoa powder, preferably Dutch-process

⅛ teaspoon salt
1 teaspoon vanilla extract

---

1. In a medium bowl, combine the yogurt, 1 cup sugar, cocoa powder, salt, and vanilla. Whisk until the sugar dissolves and the mixture is well blended, about 2 minutes. Taste and whisk in more sugar if needed. Cover and refrigerate until very cold, at least 3 hours or as long as 3 days.
2. Scrape the yogurt into the canister of an ice cream maker and freeze according to the manufacturer's directions. Eat at once or transfer to a covered container and freeze up to 4 hours.

VARIATION:

Chocolate Raspberry Swirl Frozen Yogurt

Combine 1 (10-ounce) jar no-sugar-added raspberry spreadable fruit or seedless jam with 2 tablespoons brandy or framboise and whisk to blend. Cover and refrigerate until needed. When the yogurt is at the soft-serve stage, add the raspberry mixture. Process just until swirled throughout, about 1 minute longer.

Spiced Honey-Bourbon Sauce

This is a natural with any of the honey-sweetened ice creams, such as Honey Vanilla (page 15) and Honey Peach Iced Buttermilk (page 117). But don't limit your choices, as it's also great on Speckled Vanilla Bean (page 12), Cinnamon (page 41), and Classic Chocolate (page 16).

Makes about 1¾ cups

1½ cups honey
¼ cup bourbon whisky
1 teaspoon ground cloves
⅛ teaspoon ground cinnamon

In a small bowl, combine the honey, bourbon, ground cloves, and cinnamon. Stir until well blended. The sauce can be made in advance and stored for weeks at room temperature in a covered container.

Blueberry Cinnamon Sauce

This is so good I can just eat it with a spoon. But when people are looking, I prefer it on Peaches 'n' Cream Ice Cream (page 34), Lemon Custard Ice Cream (page 36), and Earl Grey Tea Light Ice Cream (page 115).

Makes about 2 cups

---

3 cups (1½ pints) fresh blueberries, rinsed and drained, or frozen unsweetened blueberries
½ cup sugar

¼ cup water
1 tablespoon fresh lemon juice
1½ teaspoons ground cinnamon
Dash of salt

---

1. In a medium nonreactive saucepan, combine the blueberries, sugar, water, lemon juice, cinnamon, and salt.

2. Cook over low heat, stirring occasionally, until the sauce boils and thickens, about 10 minutes. If made in advance, cover and refrigerate up to 1 week. Serve warm or chilled.

Raspberry Puree

This is the classic uncooked, fat-free sauce created to enhance practically all desserts. Use this same technique to puree strawberries, blackberries, and boysenberries.

Makes about 1³/₄ cups

---

4 cups (2 pints) fresh raspberries or frozen unsweetened raspberries
¼ cup sugar, or more to taste
1 teaspoon fresh lemon juice or 2 tablespoons framboise or orange-flavored liqueur, such as Cointreau

---

1. If using fresh berries, rinse gently and drain in a colander. Pick over to remove any badly bruised or moldy fruit.
2. In a food processor or blender, puree the raspberries until smooth. Strain into a medium bowl to remove the seeds. Press through as much of the juice and fruit as you can.
3. Add ¼ cup sugar and the lemon juice; stir until the sugar dissolves, about 2 minutes. Taste and stir in more sugar if needed. Serve at once or refrigerate, covered, up to 1 week. Freeze for longer storage. Serve chilled or at room temperature.

Very Berry Sauce

This recipe works well with raspberries, boysenberries, blackberries, or a combination thereof. It is your basic cooked tart and tasty berry sauce.

Makes about 2 cups

---

4 cups fresh or frozen unsweetened raspberries, boysenberries, or blackberries, or
   a combination
½ cup sugar

2 tablespoons cornstarch
2 tablespoons water
2 teaspoons fresh lemon juice

---

1. If using fresh berries, rinse gently and drain in a colander. Pick over to remove any badly bruised or moldy fruit.

2. In a nonreactive medium saucepan, mix together the sugar and cornstarch until well blended. Stir in the berries and water. Cook over low heat, stirring, until the mixture comes to a boil. Boil gently for 1 minute.

3. Remove from the heat and stir in the lemon juice. Let cool. If made in advance, cover and refrigerate up to 3 days. Serve chilled or at room temperature.

Mango-Ginger Sauce

Mangoes may seem exotic to us, but they're quite common in other parts of the world. This makes a crowning glory for any number of frozen sweets, especially Mango-Lime Light Ice Cream (page 112), Blast-of-Chocolate Frozen Yogurt (page 123), or Coconut Ice (page 139).

Makes about 2 cups

---

3 ripe mangoes (about 12 ounces each) or half of 1 (26-ounce) jar mango slices in
  light syrup, drained
3 tablespoons sugar, or more to taste
1 tablespoon fresh lime or lemon juice
1 teaspoon grated fresh ginger

---

1. If using fresh mangoes, peel and cut away the fruit from the pits. Cut enough mango into ½-inch dice to equal ½ cup. Set aside.
2. Place the remaining mangoes in a food processor or blender with the 3 tablespoons sugar, the lime juice, and the grated ginger. Puree until smooth.
3. Pour the mango puree into a medium bowl. Taste and stir in more sugar if needed. Gently fold in the reserved diced mango. Serve at once or cover and refrigerate up to 2 days. Serve chilled.

Creamy Fruit Sauce

This recipe is the perfect "catch-all" for leftover fruits you may have on hand. Berries and other soft fruits, such as peaches or nectarines, work best. For variation, a tablespoon or two of brandy or orange-flavored liqueur makes a spirited addition.

Makes about 2 cups

---

2 cups assorted fresh fruits, cut into ¾-inch pieces if large
3 tablespoons sugar
½ cup low-fat or nonfat sour cream

---

1. In a medium bowl, combine the fruit with the sugar. Toss to coat. Let stand 1 hour.
2. In a medium bowl, whisk the sour cream to soften. Fold in the sweetened fruit. Serve at once or refrigerate, covered, up to 2 days. Serve chilled.

Chocolate Fluff

If clouds were made of chocolate, they'd probably taste like this. A generous dollop on top of your favorite ice cream may actually make you forget about hot fudge sauce . . . for a while, anyway.

Makes about 1½ cups

1 cup low-fat or nonfat sour cream
½ cup unsweetened Dutch-process cocoa
  powder
½ cup honey

1 teaspoon vanilla extract or 1 tablespoon
  brandy or rum
Dash of salt

In a medium bowl, combine the sour cream, cocoa powder, honey, vanilla, and salt. Whisk until smooth. Serve at once or cover and refrigerate up to 3 days. Serve chilled.

Chapter 4
Sorbets, Granitas, and Other Ices

Growing up, my idea of summertime heaven was a visit to my best friend's cool, dark garage on a hot afternoon. That's where her mom, Mrs. Boardman, kept a deep-freezer stocked with a seemingly endless supply of brightly colored Popsicles. We were limited to one each, of course, so Mary Ann and I thought long and hard before opening up that icy chest to check out the inventory and decide which fruity flavor would both satisfy our cravings for something sweet and exhilarating and stain our mouths for the remainder of the day.

As years passed and our tastes became more discriminating, I discovered the joy of smooth homemade sorbets and icy granitas good enough to rival any childhood memories. Sorbets, sometimes called sherbets or fruit ices, are the frozen essence of fresh fruit bound with sugar and liquid. Although high in sugar, which accounts for their silky texture, many sorbets are virtually fat-free. To balance the sugar, a little acid, such as lemon or lime juice, is added; and to prevent the mixture from freezing solid, a little bit of alcohol helps.

While developing recipes during the winter months, I was pleasantly surprised to discover canned fruits and some frozen fruits deliver consistently delicious results that often surpassed the sorbets I later made from their fresh seasonal counterparts. To prove my point, I suggest you lick the summertime blues with Apricot Sorbet d'Elisha. Other fabulous flavors, like Blood Orange Sorbet and

Cranberry Sorbet, are made from fruit juice. This should get you thinking about further experimentation, so I advise scouring health food stores and large super-markets for unusual fruit juices and blends to try.

For deep chocolate flavor without all of the fat, you'll want to add Bitter-sweet Cocoa Sorbet and its many variations to your repertoire. Go a little wild with Piña Colada and Tequila Sunrise Sorbets. Sit under the shade tree and contemplate the clean, pure taste of Green Apple Sorbet. And for more sophisti-cated endeavors, go for the Pear Sorbet with Zinfandel and Fresh Basil.

Remember that although just-made sorbet is ready to eat, it is too soft to hold the shape of a scoop. For the ultimate flavor and texture, store sorbet in the freezer for at least 1 hour prior to serving.

The granular Italian ice called granita is far less sweet than sorbet, but equally rejuvenating. Homemade granitas were traditionally made by pouring the flavored liquid into a shallow pan and placing it in the freezer. You would then follow a tedious series of steps where the frozen ice is scraped with the tines of a fork and refrozen to acquire just the right texture. The good news for granita lovers is that your ice cream maker delivers instant gratification. Serve granitas directly from the ma-chine and savor those flavored ice crystals. In the unlikely event that there is any left over, let it freeze solid, then break into large chunks and process in the food processor.

These recipes will teach you to wake up your taste buds with an Espresso Granita and end the day with a Frozen Gin and Tonic. Lovers of the tart-and-tangy will no doubt opt for Lemon Granita with its lively, thirst-quenching proper-ties, and how about some Sangria Granita after lunch?

Green Apple Sorbet

This unusual sorbet has a pleasantly coarse texture and a vibrant, fresh apple flavor. Peel the apples if you like, but I think the little flecks of green add to the appearance.

Makes about 3 cups

1½ pounds tart green apples (about 3 large), such as Granny Smith, cored and coarsely chopped

½ cup apple juice or apple cider

¾ cup sugar

2 tablespoons fresh lemon juice

1 tablespoon applejack, Calvados, or vodka

---

1. In a food processor or blender, puree the apples and apple juice until smooth. Transfer to a large bowl.

2. Add the sugar, lemon juice, and applejack to the apple puree. Stir to blend well. Cover and refrigerate until very cold, at least 2 hours or as long as 1 day.

3. Stir the mixture to blend and pour into the canister of an ice cream maker. Freeze according to the manufacturer's directions. Transfer to a covered container and freeze until firm, at least 1 hour or as long as 3 days.

Apricot Sorbet d'Elisha

Elisha Glickman, my eight-year-old sous-chef *and tireless taster, knowingly declared this sorbet "the best." You may agree with her when you see how fresh tasting canned apricots can be.*

Makes about 3 cups

---

2 (16-ounce) cans apricot halves in heavy syrup
¾ cup sugar
2 tablespoons fresh lemon juice
1 tablespoon amaretto or brandy

---

1. Drain the apricots, reserving ½ cup of the syrup.
2. In a food processor or blender, puree the apricots until smooth. Transfer to a large bowl.
3. Add the reserved ½ cup syrup, the sugar, lemon juice, and amaretto to the apricot puree. Whisk to blend. Cover and refrigerate until very cold, at least 2 hours or as long as 3 days.
4. Whisk the mixture to blend and pour into the canister of an ice cream maker. Freeze according to the manufacturer's directions. Transfer to a covered container and freeze until firm, at least 1 hour or as long as 3 days.

Banana Sorbet

Did you love frozen chocolate-covered bananas when you were a kid? Drizzle a bit of Homemade Chocolate Syrup (page 88) over this sorbet and see if it reminds you of anything. By the way, when bananas are overripe, their skins should be speckled brown.

Makes about 3 cups

---

4 overripe medium-size bananas
½ cup cold water
¾ cup sugar

2 tablespoons fresh lemon juice
1 tablespoon rum or vodka

---

1. In a food processor or blender, puree the bananas with the water until smooth. Pour into a large bowl.

2. Add the sugar, lemon juice, and rum to the banana puree. Whisk to blend. Cover and refrigerate until very cold, at least 2 hours or as long as 3 days.

3. Whisk the mixture to blend and pour into the canister of an ice cream maker. Freeze according to the manufacturer's directions. Transfer to a covered container and freeze until firm, at least 1 hour or as long as 3 days.

Bittersweet Cocoa Sorbet

This intensely chocolate sorbet reminds me of a frozen chocolate mousse—minus a few hundred of the usual calories. It's delightful on its own, but a drizzle of Raspberry Puree (page 126) and a few Chocolate Curls and Twirls (page 93) on top will make it a worthy finale to any dinner party. Best of all, it costs considerably less than any commercially produced chocolate sorbet.

Makes about 1 quart

1½ cups sugar
¾ cup unsweetened Dutch-process cocoa
   powder
⅛ teaspoon salt

3 cups water
3 tablespoons light corn syrup
½ teaspoon vanilla extract

---

1. In a medium nonreactive saucepan, combine the sugar, cocoa powder, and salt. Whisk to blend. Gradually whisk in the water until the mixture is well blended. Whisk in the corn syrup.

2. Cook over medium heat, whisking occasionally, until the sugar dissolves and the mixture is smooth, 2 to 3 minutes. Remove from the heat and let cool to room temperature. Stir in the vanilla. Cover and refrigerate until very cold, at least 2 hours or as long as 3 days.

3. Whisk the mixture to blend and pour into the canister of an ice cream maker. Freeze according to the manufacturer's directions. Transfer to a covered container and freeze until firm, at least 1 hour or as long as 3 days.

VARIATIONS:

Dark Mocha Sorbet

Substitute 3 cups brewed strong coffee for the water, or add 1 tablespoon instant coffee granules with the cocoa powder.

Mexican Chocolate Sorbet

Add 2 teaspoons instant coffee granules and ¼ teaspoon ground cinnamon with the cocoa powder. When the mixture is at the soft-serve stage, add 1 tablespoon dark run.

Chocolate Orange Sorbet

Add ¼ teaspoon orange extract with the vanilla. Taste for flavoring. Add more orange extract if needed, a few drops at a time.

Chocolate Mint Sorbet

Add ¼ teaspoon peppermint extract with the vanilla. Taste for flavoring. Add more peppermint extract if needed, a few drops at a time.

Blueberry Sorbet

For a double dose of blueberries, spoon some Blueberry Cinnamon Sauce (page 125) over each serving.

Makes about 3 cups

---

3 cups (1½ pints) fresh blueberries, rinsed and drained, or frozen unsweetened blueberries, thawed
½ cup water

1 cup sugar
2 tablespoons fresh lemon juice
1 tablespoon vodka

---

1. In a food processor or blender, puree the blueberries with the water until smooth. Pour the mixture into a large bowl.

2. Add the sugar, lemon juice, and vodka to the blueberry puree. Whisk to blend. Cover and refrigerate until very cold, at least 2 hours or as long as 3 days.

3. Whisk the mixture to blend and pour into the canister of an ice cream maker. Freeze according to the manufacturer's directions. Transfer to a covered container and freeze until firm, at least 1 hour or as long as 3 days.

Coconut Ice

To highlight the Southeast Asian overtones of this snow-white ice, ladle a bit of Mango-Ginger Sauce (page 128) over the top. Or for a more American approach, simply drizzle with Homemade Chocolate Syrup (page 88) and sprinkle with chopped peanuts or toasted coconut. Just be sure to make this with regular or low-fat unsweetened coconut milk, not canned coconut cream.

Makes about 3½ cups

---

2 (13½-ounce) cans unsweetened coconut milk

1 cup sugar

1½ tablespoons fresh lime or lemon juice

1 tablespoon rum or vodka

⅛ teaspoon salt

---

1. In a large bowl, whisk the coconut milk to blend evenly. Whisk in the sugar, lime juice, rum, and salt. Cover and refrigerate until very cold, at least 2 hours or as long as 3 days.

2. Whisk the mixture to blend and pour into the canister of an ice cream maker. Freeze according to the manufacturer's directions. Transfer to a covered container and freeze until firm, at least 1 hour or as long as 3 days.

Cranberry Sorbet

Cranberry juice makes a sweet-tart sorbet with rich ruby color. For a slight flavor variation, use one of the juice blends, such as cranberry-raspberry or cranberry-apple. And for special occasions, scoop into stemmed glasses and top with a splash of chilled champagne or vodka just before serving.

Makes about 3 cups

---

2 cups (16 ounces) cranberry juice
¾ cup sugar
2 tablespoons fresh lemon juice
1 tablespoon vodka

---

1. In a large bowl, combine the cranberry juice, sugar, lemon juice, and vodka. Whisk to blend. Cover and refrigerate until very cold, at least 2 hours or as long as 3 days.
2. Whisk the mixture to blend and pour into the canister of an ice cream maker. Freeze according to the manufacturer's directions. Transfer to a covered container and freeze until firm, at least 1 hour or as long as 3 days.

Pink Grapefruit Sorbet with Campari Splash

The bittersweet flavors of grapefruit juice and Campari, an Italian aperitif, are mellowed by the cool, refreshing taste of mint. Serve this as a light dessert or as the traditional "palate cleanser" between the courses of a formal dinner.

Makes about 3 cups

---

2 cups pink or red grapefruit juice, fresh
(from 2 to 3 grapefruit) or from
concentrate
1 cup sugar

1 tablespoon Campari or vodka
Campari-Mint Syrup (recipe follows)
Fresh mint sprigs, for garnish

---

1. In a large bowl, combine the grapefruit juice, sugar, and Campari. Whisk to blend. Cover and refrigerate until very cold, at least 2 hours or as long as 3 days.
2. Whisk the mixture to blend and pour into the canister of an ice cream maker. Freeze according to the manufacturer's directions. Transfer to a covered container and freeze until firm, at least 1 hour or as long as 3 days.
3. To serve, scoop the sorbet into stemmed glasses or dessert dishes. Drizzle about 1½ tablespoons Campari-Mint Syrup over each serving and garnish with a sprig of fresh mint.

Campari-Mint Syrup

Makes about ⅔ cup

½ cup sugar
½ cup water
3 to 4 tablespoons Campari
1 tablespoon chopped fresh mint leaves

1. In a small heavy saucepan, combine the sugar and water. Bring to a boil over medium heat, stirring to dissolve the sugar. Reduce the heat to low and simmer 10 minutes without stirring. Remove from the heat and let cool to room temperature.

2. Stir in 3 tablespoons Campari and the mint. Taste, adding more Campari if needed. Cover and refrigerate until very cold, at least 2 hours or as long as 2 days.

Kiwi-Lime Sorbet

Be very careful when you puree kiwifruit in the food processor. If the tiny black seeds are broken, the mixture will turn from lovely pale green to olive drab.

Makes about 3½ cups

1½ pounds ripe kiwifruit (about 8 large kiwi), peeled and coarsely chopped
1 cup sugar, or more to taste
¼ cup fresh lime juice
1 tablespoon vodka

---

1. In a food processor, combine the kiwi, 1 cup sugar, the lime juice, and the vodka. Puree, pulsing on and off, until the mixture is just smooth. Do not overprocess.
2. Transfer the kiwi puree to a large bowl. Taste for sweetness; stir in more sugar, 1 tablespoon at a time, if needed. Cover and refrigerate until very cold, at least 2 hours or as long as 3 days.
3. Gently stir the mixture to blend and pour into the canister of an ice cream machine. Freeze according to the manufacturer's directions. Transfer to a covered container and freeze until firm, at least 1 hour or as long as 3 days.

Mango Margarita Sorbet

Canned frozen limeade concentrate delivers a tart and zesty flavor that matches the intensity of the mango without overwhelming it.

Makes about 3½ cups

---

3 ripe medium mangoes (about 12 ounces each), or half of 1 (26-ounce) jar mango slices in light syrup, drained

¾ cup sugar

¼ cup thawed limeade concentrate, undiluted

2 tablespoons tequila

1 tablespoon orange liqueur, such as Triple Sec

Dash of salt

---

1. If using fresh mangoes, peel them and cut the fruit from the large flat pit. In a food processor or blender, puree the mango until smooth. Transfer to a large bowl.

2. Add the sugar, limeade concentrate, tequila, orange liqueur, and salt to the mango puree. Whisk to blend. Cover and refrigerate until very cold, at least 2 hours or as long as 3 days.

3. Whisk the mixture to blend and pour into the canister of an ice cream maker. Freeze according to the manufacturer's directions. Transfer to a covered container and freeze until firm, at least 1 hour or as long as 3 days.

Blood Orange Sorbet

Blood oranges, with their deep burgundy-splashed flesh, are becoming increasingly available in this country. I use them for their dramatic crimson color; but when they're not in season, Valencia or navel oranges work just as well.

Makes about 3 cups

---

3 pounds blood oranges (8 to 10 medium oranges)
1 cup sugar
1 tablespoon fresh lemon juice
1 tablespoon orange liqueur, such as Triple Sec, or vodka

---

1. Rinse and dry 1 or 2 of the oranges and grate 2 teaspoons of zest from their skins.
2. Squeeze 2 cups of juice from the oranges. Strain to remove any seeds.
3. In a large bowl, combine the orange zest, orange juice, sugar, lemon juice, and liqueur. Whisk to blend. Cover and refrigerate until very cold, at least 2 hours or as long as 3 days.
4. Whisk the mixture to blend and pour into the canister of an ice cream maker. Freeze according to the manufacturer's directions. Transfer to a covered container and freeze until firm, at least 1 hour or as long as 3 days.

Pear Sorbet with Zinfandel and Fresh Basil

Even if it sounds a little weird to you, please trust me on this one. Sweet basil leaves lend their spicy perfume to the classic pairing of pears and red wine, making an original and very pleasing combination.

Makes about 1 quart

---

3 (16-ounce) cans sliced Bartlett pears in heavy syrup, drained
1½ cups Zinfandel Syrup (recipe follows)
4 to 6 fresh basil leaves, finely chopped
Basil flowers and/or leaves for garnish

---

1. In a food processor or blender, puree the pears until smooth. Pour into a large bowl.
2. Stir in 1 cup of the Zinfandel Syrup and the chopped basil leaves. Cover and refrigerate until very cold, at least 2 hours or as long as 2 days.
3. Stir the mixture to blend and pour into the canister of an ice cream maker. Freeze according to the manufacturer's directions. Transfer to a covered container and freeze until firm, at least 1 hour or as long as 3 days.
4. To serve, scoop the pear sorbet into stemmed glasses or dessert dishes. Drizzle 1 or 2 tablespoons of the remaining Zinfandel Syrup over each serving and garnish with fresh basil.

Zinfandel Syrup

Makes about 1½ cups

1½ cups Zinfandel or other fruity red wine
¾ cup sugar
1 (2 × ½-inch) strip lemon zest
4 large fresh basil leaves

---

1. In a nonreactive medium saucepan, combine the wine, sugar, lemon zest, and whole basil leaves. Bring to a boil over medium heat, stirring to dissolve the sugar. Reduce the heat to medium-low and simmer 10 minutes without stirring.

2. Strain the syrup into a medium bowl, discarding the lemon zest and basil leaves. Let cool to room temperature, then cover and refrigerate. The syrup can be made in advance and stored for weeks in a covered jar in the refrigerator.

Peaches Bellini Sorbet

Pour Italian sparkling wine or champagne over a scoop of peach sorbet for a taste of the good life, Italian-style. I've suggested a full bottle of sparkling wine to allow for refills at the table, but a split would be plenty. Almond biscotti go beautifully on the side.

Makes about 3½ cups

1½ pounds ripe peaches (about 6 medium), peeled and pitted, or 3 cups frozen unsweetened peach slices, thawed
½ cup cold water
1 cup sugar

2 tablespoons fresh lemon juice
1 tablespoon peach brandy
1 bottle (750 ml) Prosecco or other sparkling wine, well chilled

---

1. In a food processor or blender, puree the peaches with water until smooth. Pour into a large bowl.

2. Add the sugar, lemon juice, and peach brandy to the peach puree. Stir to blend. Cover and refrigerate until very cold, at least 2 hours or as long as 3 days.

3. Stir the mixture to blend and pour into the canister of an ice cream maker. Freeze according to the manufacturer's directions. Transfer to a covered container and freeze until firm, at least 1 hour or as long as 3 days.

4. To serve, scoop the sorbet into 4 to 6 chilled champagne flutes. Pour several tablespoons of sparkling wine over each dish and serve at once. Pass the rest of the bottle for refills.

Persimmon Sorbet

Whole ripe persimmons can be frozen up to 6 months, which extends their season considerably. To use, let them thaw about 15 minutes at room temperature before cutting in half and scooping out the pulp. In addition to its brilliant orange color, persimmon sorbet has a full-bodied, texture, which makes it unique. The tomato-shaped Fuyu persimmon is crisp when ripe, but the larger, teardrop-shaped Hachiya persimmon is ripe only when jelly-soft.

Makes about 3½ cups

---

8 large, very ripe Hachiya persimmons	1 tablespoon fresh lemon juice
½ cup water	1 tablespoon orange liqueur, such
¾ cup sugar	as Triple Sec, or vodka

---

1. Cut the persimmons in half lengthwise and scoop the flesh into a food processor. Discard the skin and any seeds. Puree the pulp and transfer to a medium bowl. (There should be about 2 cups puree.)

2. Add the water, sugar, lemon juice, and orange liqueur to the persimmon puree. Stir to blend well. Cover and refrigerate until very cold, at least 2 hours or as long as 3 days.

3. Stir the mixture to blend and pour into the canister of an ice cream maker. Freeze according to the manufacturer's directions. Transfer to a covered container and freeze until firm, at least 1 hour or as long as 3 days.

Plum Good Sorbet

Sweet plum wine perks up the flavor of ripe red plums. For a delicious extravagance, use some of the leftover wine from the bottle to macerate fresh strawberries: it leaves them with a lovely sheen and imparts a bit of sweetness.

Makes about 3 cups

2¼ pounds ripe red or black-skinned plums (10 to 12), such as Santa Rosa, cut in half and pitted
1 cup sugar
½ cup water

¼ cup Japanese plum wine or other sweet wine
1 (3-inch) cinnamon stick
1 tablespoon fresh lemon juice

---

1. In a nonreactive medium saucepan, combine the plums, sugar, water, plum wine, and cinnamon stick. Cook over medium heat, stirring occasionally, until the sugar dissolves and the plums are very soft, about 15 minutes.

2. Strain the mixture through a sieve into a large bowl, pressing through as much of the fruit as you can. Discard the cinnamon stick, plum skins, and any stringy fibers. Let the plum puree cool to room temperature. Stir in the lemon juice. Cover and refrigerate until very cold, at least 2 hours or as long as 3 days.

3. Stir the mixture to blend and pour into the canister of an ice cream maker. Freeze according to the manufacturer's directions. Transfer to a covered container and freeze until firm, at least 1 hour or as long as 3 days.

Spiced Raspberry Sorbet

Red wine adds a very grown-up character to raspberries. Toss in a few spices and liqueurs and voilà! You have a sophisticated sorbet, ideal for entertaining.

Makes about 3½ cups

---

2 cups (1 pint) fresh raspberries or frozen unsweetened raspberries

1½ cups fruity dry red wine, such as Zinfandel

1 cup sugar

1 (3-inch) cinnamon stick

1 whole clove

1 tablespoon fresh lemon juice

1 tablespoon orange liqueur, such as Triple Sec

1 tablespoon framboise or raspberry liqueur, such as Chambord

---

1. In a heavy nonreactive medium saucepan, combine the raspberries, wine, sugar, cinnamon stick, and clove. Bring to a boil over medium heat. Reduce the heat to low and simmer 15 minutes. Remove from the heat. Pour into a large bowl and let cool to room temperature.

2. Stir the lemon juice, orange liqueur, and framboise into the cooled raspberry-wine syrup. Cover and refrigerate until very cold, at least 2 hours or as long as 3 days.

3. Strain the syrup into a pitcher or bowl, discarding the raspberry seeds, cinnamon stick, and clove. Immediately pour into an ice cream maker and freeze according to the manufacturer's directions. Transfer to a covered container and freeze until firm, at least 1 hour or as long as 3 days.

Watermelon Sorbet

I love watermelon, but I don't like the fact that a large one can consume almost an entire shelf of my refrigerator before it's finally eaten. So here's the answer: enjoy the fresh taste of watermelon in the form of sorbet directly from your freezer. Sometimes I scatter a few miniature semisweet chocolate chips over each serving to resemble watermelon seeds.

Makes about 3 cups

---

1 (2½-pound) piece of watermelon, rind and seeds discarded, flesh cut into chunks (about 4 cups)
1 cup sugar
2 tablespoons fresh lemon juice
1 tablespoon vodka

---

1. In a food processor or blender, puree the watermelon until smooth. Transfer to a medium bowl.
2. Add the sugar, lemon juice, and vodka to the watermelon puree. Stir to blend. Cover and refrigerate until very cold, at least 2 hours or as long as 3 days.
3. Stir the mixture to blend and pour into the canister of an ice cream maker. Freeze according to the manufacturer's directions. Transfer to a covered container and freeze until firm, at least 1 hour or as long as 3 days.

Piña Colada Sorbet

Canned pineapple enjoys a spirited boost from coconut milk and rum, making a tropical sorbet that is both complex in flavor and very refreshing. Just for fun, serve in a stemmed glass with a little paper umbrella. Take a bite and close your eyes; soon you'll be wiggling your toes in the warm sand.

Makes about 1 quart

---

2 (20-ounce) cans crushed pineapple in heavy syrup, drained, syrup reserved

⅓ cup canned unsweetened coconut milk

⅓ cup sugar

2 tablespoons light rum

1 tablespoon fresh lemon juice

---

1. In a food processor or blender, puree the pineapple until smooth.

2. Pour the puree into a large bowl. Add the reserved pineapple syrup, coconut milk, sugar, rum, and lemon juice. Stir to blend well. Cover and refrigerate until very cold, at least 2 hours or as long as 3 days.

3. Stir the mixture to blend and pour into the canister of an ice cream maker. Freeze according to the manufacturer's directions. Transfer to a covered container and freeze until firm, at least 1 hour or as long as 3 days.

Strawberry Daiquiri Sorbet

Be sure to taste fresh strawberries before using them. If you're lucky enough to have some that are as sweet as candy, reduce the sugar in this recipe by two tablespoons.

Makes about 3 cups

---

4 cups (2 pints) fresh strawberries, rinsed and hulled, or frozen unsweetened strawberries, thawed
1 cup sugar
2 tablespoons light rum
1½ tablespoons fresh lime juice

---

1. In a food processor or blender, puree the strawberries until smooth. Strain to remove the seeds, if desired.
2 Transfer the puree to a medium bowl and add the sugar, rum, and lime juice. Whisk to blend well. Cover and refrigerate until very cold, at least 2 hours or as long as 3 days.
3. Whisk the mixture to blend and pour into the canister of an ice cream maker. Freeze according to the manufacturer's directions. Transfer to a covered container and freeze until firm, at least 1 hour or as long as 3 days.

Sorbets, Granitas, and Other Ices

Tequila Sunrise Sorbet

This won't have the dramatic layered effect of its namesake cocktail, but the flavor is definitely there. To serve, drizzle with additional grenadine and garnish with a fresh mint sprig.

Makes about 3 cups

---

2 cups orange juice, fresh or from
   concentrate
¾ cup sugar
2 tablespoons grenadine syrup

2 tablespoons tequila
1 tablespoon fresh lime juice

---

1. In a large bowl, combine the orange juice, sugar, grenadine, tequila, and lime juice. Whisk to blend. Cover and refrigerate until very cold, at least 2 hours or as long as 3 days.
2. Whisk the mixture to blend and pour into the canister of an ice cream maker. Freeze according to the manufacturer's directions. Transfer to a covered container and freeze until firm, at least 1 hour or as long as 3 days.

Frozen Gin and Tonic

There's nothing like a tart gin and tonic to refresh guests on a hot summer day. Try serving this icy edible version with a wedge of lime in tall frosted glasses, with long-handled iced tea spoons. Because of the amount of gin, this sorbet will not freeze hard and should be consumed as soon as it is ready.

Makes about 1 quart

⅔ cup sugar
⅓ cup gin
¼ cup fresh lime juice

4 teaspoons grated lime zest
1 (28-ounce) bottle tonic water

---

1. In a large bowl, combine the sugar, gin, lime juice, and lime zest. Stir to blend and dissolve the sugar.
2. Gradually stir in the tonic water. Cover and refrigerate until very cold, at least 2 hours or as long as 3 days.
3. Stir the mixture to blend and pour into the canister of an ice cream maker. Freeze according to the manufacturer's directions. Eat at once.

Cherry Granita

Iced fresh cherries are always irresistible, so you know this can't help but be good. A few Chocolate Curls and Twirls (page 93) scattered on top make it even better.

Makes about 1 quart

¾ pound fresh sweet cherries or 1½ cups frozen unsweetened Bing cherries
¾ cup sugar
¾ cup water
1 tablespoon fresh lemon juice

---

1. If using fresh cherries, remove any stems. Rinse well and pat dry with paper towels. Working over a heavy medium saucepan to catch the juices, cut the cherries in half with a small stainless steel knife. Cut out the pit with the tip of the knife and drop the cherries into the saucepan. If using frozen cherries, place them directly in the saucepan.
2. Add the sugar and water to the saucepan. Bring to a boil over medium heat, stirring occasionally. Reduce the heat to low and simmer until the sugar is dissolved and the cherries are tender, 5 to 7 minutes. Let cool to room temperature. Stir in the lemon juice.
3. Transfer the mixture to the bowl of a food processor and puree until smooth. Pass though a food mill or strain through a sieve into a medium bowl, pressing through as much fruit and juice as possible. Cover and refrigerate until very cold, at least 2 hours or as long as 3 days.
4. Stir the mixture to blend and pour into the canister of an ice cream maker. Freeze according to the manufacturer's directions. Eat at once.

Lemon Granita

Italians are renowned for their sweet-tart fruit ices, made with only enough sugar to accent the natural fruit flavor. If you can find Meyer lemons, which are exceptionally sweet, the flavor will be superior, but any variety will do. A ripe red strawberry on the side makes a striking garnish, and a splash of crème de cassis over each serving turns this into an adult sno-cone.

Makes about 1 quart

1½ cups cold water
½ cup fresh lemon juice (from about 3 lemons)
⅓ cup sugar or honey

---

1. In a medium bowl, combine the water, lemon juice, and sugar. Stir to dissolve the sugar. Refrigerate until very cold, at least 2 hours or as long as 3 days.
2. Stir the mixture to blend and pour into the canister of an ice cream maker. Freeze according to the manufacturer's directions. Eat at once.

Raspberry Granita

Since raspberries vary greatly in sweetness, you really do have to taste here and adjust the sugar accordingly. Other berries can be used with the same process.

Makes about 1 quart

1½ cups (about ½ pound) fresh
   or frozen unsweetened raspberries
¾ cup water
⅓ to ½ cup sugar
1 tablespoon fresh lemon juice

---

1. In a food processor or blender, combine the raspberries and water. Puree until smooth. Strain through a sieve into a medium bowl, pressing through as much fruit and juice as possible. Discard the seeds.

2. Add ⅓ cup sugar and the lemon juice. Stir to blend and dissolve the sugar. Taste for sweetness and add more sugar, 1 tablespoon at a time, if needed. Cover and refrigerate until very cold, at least 2 hours or as long as 3 days.

3. Stir the mixture to blend and pour into the canister of an ice cream maker. Freeze according to the manufacturer's directions. Eat at once.

Root Beer Granita

Served in a frosty mug with a scoop of Voluptuous Vanilla Ice Cream (page 14), this makes the ultimate root beer float.

Makes about 1 quart

---

2 cups (16 ounces) root beer
¼ cup sugar

---

1. In a medium bowl, combine the root beer and sugar. Stir to dissolve the sugar. Cover and refrigerate until very cold, at least 2 hours or as long as 3 days.
2. Stir the mixture to blend and pour into the canister of an ice cream maker. Freeze according to the manufacturer's directions. Eat at once.

Sangria Granita

With the advent of wine snobbery, sangria, a Spanish blend of wine, brandy, and assorted fruits, seemed to go out of fashion. You'll find that in a frozen state, however, these flavors are a big hit. I like to serve this with fresh strawberries and slices of ripe honeydew melon.

Makes about 1 quart

---

1 (12-ounce) can lemon-lime soda
1 cup fruity dry red wine, such as
  Zinfandel
½ cup sugar

½ cup orange juice, fresh or from
  concentrate
1 tablespoon brandy

---

1. In a large bowl, combine the soda, wine, sugar, orange juice, and brandy. Whisk to blend. Cover and refrigerate until very cold, at least 2 hours or as long as 3 days.
2. Whisk the mixture to blend and pour into the canister of an ice cream maker. Freeze according to the manufacturer's directions. Eat at once.

Espresso Granita

Serve this in demitasse cups with a twist of lemon as a garnish. It can be dressed up, too, with a shot of brandy over each serving and a dollop of whipped cream.

Makes about 1 quart

---

2 cups freshly brewed espresso or strong coffee
¼ cup sugar

---

1. In a medium bowl, combine the hot coffee and sugar. Stir to dissolve the sugar. Let cool to room temperature. Cover and refrigerate until very cold, at least 2 hours or as long as 3 days.

2. Whisk the mixture to blend and pour into the canister of an ice cream maker. Freeze according to the manufacturer's directions. Eat at once.

VARIATIONS:

Café Latte Granita

Add 1 cup milk to the coffee and sugar mixture.

Spirited Espresso Granita

Add 1 tablespoon liqueur, such as Sambuca or Kahlúa, to the coffee and sugar mixture.

Irish Breakfast Tea Granita

I happen to love Irish Breakfast tea, so while that was my choice for this icy delight, any other flavorful black tea will work just as well. For the granita, be sure to brew the tea a little stronger than you would for sipping.

Makes about 1 quart

---

2 cups freshly brewed Irish Breakfast tea
⅓ cup sugar or honey
2 tablespoons fresh lemon juice

---

1. In a medium bowl, combine the hot tea with the sugar or honey. Stir to dissolve the sugar. Stir in the lemon juice. Let cool to room temperature. Cover and refrigerate until very cold, at least 2 hours or as long as 3 days.
2. Stir the mixture to blend and pour into the canister of an ice cream maker. Freeze according to the manufacturer's directions. Eat at once.

Chapter 5

Ice Cream Cakes and Other Frozen Desserts

Everyone knows there's something special about an ice cream cake, that tantalizing juxtaposition of flavors and textures, ice cold, perfectly sweet. What fun to discover how easy it is to make these cakes and other assembled frozen desserts at home. Now that you've mastered the art of making ice creams and sorbets, you'll want to "show your stuff" for parties and other special occasions. So here's the scoop: the recipes in this chapter, designed to please both the eye and the palate, are sure to delight your guests.

When you make the ice cream from scratch in your ice cream maker, you get to choose exactly which flavors you'd like. And for convenience, to save time if you prefer, many of these frozen confections can be made with store-bought equivalents. However you assemble them, the real celebration is knowing that a stunning dessert, made at your leisure, is tucked away in the freezer. Whether you wow guests with Fudgy Strawberry Charlotte or Chocolate Apricot Cream Pavé or start them giggling over the whimsical Frozen Italian Fantasy, which resembles spaghetti and meatballs, or Deep-Dish Brownie Pizza, dessert from the freezer is guaranteed to be a memorable occasion.

Ice cream cakes and pies, garnished to perfection, taste terrific and often look like the work of an accomplished pastry chef. Best of all, they can be assembled long before the guests arrive. Pop an Ice Cream Bonbon in your mouth while you ponder whether to serve Coffee Toffee Ice Cream Mud Pie or Peachy Angel Food Tunnel Cake to the bridge club. End your Thanksgiving feast with Frozen Pumpkin Pie Deluxe. Celebrate good report cards with Lickety-Split Ice Cream Sandwiches. Here you'll find an ice cream dessert for just about every occasion.

Totally Cool Tips

- Many of the recipes in this chapter say to let the ice cream soften slightly before packing it into the mold or the crust. The ice cream should still be quite firm, but just manageable enough to scoop or spread as directed. If the ice cream is allowed to melt or becomes very soft, ice crystals will form when it is refrozen. This simple mistake could ruin the texture of your beautiful dessert.
- "Flash freezing" desserts will keep your garnishes intact. Freeze the dessert uncovered until firm to the touch, then place in an airtight container or wrap in plastic wrap and freeze until serving time.
- To make cutting or spooning easier, soften frozen desserts 5 to 10 minutes at room temperature or 15 to 20 minutes in the refrigerator just before serving. Once individual portions are served, the ice cream will soften quickly.
- When serving frozen desserts, dip the knife or spoon in hot water and quickly blot dry with a towel before slicing or scooping *each serving*.
- Serve ice cream desserts on chilled plates or dishes to slow the melting process.

Chocolate Apricot Cream Pavé

This dessert, layered like bricks and mortar, gets its name from the French word for paving stone. But that's where the resemblance ends. With ribbons of sorbet and frozen yogurt, there's nothing "heavy" here.

Serves 8 to 10

---

1 (15-ounce) prepared chocolate loaf cake
⅓ cup apricot brandy
2 cups Honey Vanilla Frozen Yogurt (page 122) or store-bought honey vanilla frozen yogurt, softened slightly

2 cups Apricot Sorbet d'Elisha (page 134) or store-bought apricot sorbet, softened slightly
1½ cups Chocolate Fluff (page 130) or whipped cream

---

1. Freeze the cake until firm, about 30 minutes. (This will make slicing easier.) Using a long serrated knife, cut the cake horizontally into 5 equal layers. Lay the cake slices in a single layer on a clean work surface and brush with apricot brandy. Set the top layer aside.

2. Working quickly, spread 2 slices of cake each with an even layer of 1 cup frozen yogurt; coat the 2 other slices each with an even layer of 1 cup apricot sorbet, smoothing the edges with a small spoon or your fingertips.

3. Using a large metal spatula or pancake turner to lift each piece, place 1 cake slice on a serving plate, yogurt-side up. Top with a sorbet layer, sorbet-side up. Repeat, alternating the remaining 2 layers. Place the reserved cake top over the final layer of sorbet, pressing gently to sandwich the layers. Align the layers with your hands to straighten the sides, if necessary. Cover tightly and freeze until firm, at least 6 hours.

4. To serve, let the pavé stand at room temperature for 10 minutes to soften. Cut into slices ¾ inch thick with a long-handled knife dipped in hot water. Serve on chilled dessert plates, with a dollop of Chocolate Fluff or whipped cream.

Black and White Birthday Ice Cream Cake

Every birthday deserves cake and ice cream. This two-in-one recipe, covered with swirls of whipped cream, tops a fudgy layer of chocolate mousse cake with your favorite ice cream. The finished cake can be drizzled with chocolate sauce, topped with berries, or sprinkled with festive garnishes as you like; but the only last-minute touch really required is birthday candles.

Serves 10 to 12

---

6 ounces bittersweet or semisweet
   chocolate
6 tablespoons unsalted butter
6 eggs, separated
¾ cup sugar
1 teaspoon vanilla extract

⅛ teaspoon cream of tartar
1 quart Bittersweet Chocolate Truffle Ice
   Cream (page 18) or other ice cream of
   choice
1 cup heavy cream
¼ cup sifted powdered sugar

---

1. Preheat the oven to 325°F. Lightly butter and flour a 9-inch springform pan. In a small heavy saucepan, melt the chocolate and butter over low heat, stirring until smooth. In a large bowl, beat the egg yolks with ½ cup of the sugar until light and fluffy, about 5 minutes. Gradually beat in the warm chocolate mixture and the vanilla.

2. In another large bowl, beat the egg whites with the cream of tartar until soft peaks form. Gradually add the remaining ¼ cup sugar, 1 tablespoon at a time. Continue beating until the egg whites form stiff but glossy peaks. Fold the egg whites into the chocolate mixture until well incorporated.

3. Pour the batter into the prepared pan and bake until the top is just set and the edges begin to pull away from the sides of the pan, about 35 minutes. (The center will still be quite soft.) Place the cake on a wire rack to cool completely. The center of the cake will fall as it cools.

4. Soften the ice cream for 5 minutes at room temperature or 3 seconds on High in the microwave. Spoon the ice cream evenly over the cake in the springform pan, pressing down to remove any air pockets. Cover and freeze until firm, at least 4 hours or overnight.

5. In a large mixing bowl, combine the cream and powdered sugar. Beat with an electric mixer on medium speed until soft peaks form.

6. Place the springform pan on a chilled serving plate. Run a thin knife along the sides of the pan to free the sides. Release the sides of the pan. Working quickly, spoon or pipe the whipped cream over the sides and top of the cake. Freeze until firm to the touch, about 30 minutes. Wrap in plastic wrap and freeze at least 6 hours or as long as 3 days. To serve, let thaw 10 to 15 minutes in the refrigerator. Cut into wedges with a sharp knife dipped in hot water.

Deep-Dish Brownie Pizza

This may just be the last word in chocolate decadence. It can serve as a great cake-and-ice cream dessert for a birthday party . . . for little kids from 6 to 60. To make this even easier, use two of your favorite flavors of store-brought ice cream.

Serves 10 to 12

1 pound bittersweet or semisweet chocolate, chopped
4 tablespoons unsalted butter
¼ cup unsweetened cocoa powder
5 eggs
1½ cups sugar
1½ teaspoons vanilla extract
1 cup flour
½ teaspoon baking powder

⅛ teaspoon salt
1 cup semisweet chocolate chips (6 ounces)
3 cups White Chocolate Ice Cream (page 21), softened slightly
3 cups Rocky Road Ice Cream (page 33) or store-bought
1½ cups Hot Fudge Sauce (page 82)
Chocolate sprinkles

1. Preheat the oven to 325°F. Generously grease a 16-inch pizza pan.
2. Melt the chocolate and butter in a double boiler over low heat, stirring, until smooth. Stir in the cocoa powder until well blended. Remove from the heat and let cool to tepid.
3. In a large mixer bowl, beat the eggs and sugar with an electric mixer until thickened and pale yellow. Stir in the vanilla and the chocolate mixture to blend well.
4. Combine the flour, baking powder, and salt and sift into the chocolate mixture, stirring just to combine. Fold in the chocolate chips. Spread the batter in the prepared pizza pan, leaving at least a ½-inch border around the edges to allow for expansion.
5. Bake until the edges are set and moist crumbs adhere to a toothpick inserted in the

center, 35 to 40 minutes. (The center will still be quite soft.) Let cool completely. (The brownie crust can be made in advance and stored airtight for 2 days or frozen.)

6. Spread an even layer of White Chocolate Ice Cream over the crust, leaving a ½-inch border around the edges. Top with small scoops of Rocky Road Ice Cream and drizzle with Hot Fudge Sauce. Garnish with chocolate sprinkles. Freeze until firm to the touch, about 30 minutes. Cover and freeze at least 4 hours or as long as 3 days. Let stand 10 to 15 minutes in the refrigerator before cutting into wedges to serve.

Peachy Angel Food Tunnel Cake

Make your own angel food cake with leftover egg whites, buy one from a bakery, or use a cake mix. For this recipe it's easiest to start with a cake that is partially frozen.

Serves 8 to 10

---

1 (13-ounce) 9- or 10-inch tube angel food cake

¼ cup peach brandy

2 tablespoons water

1½ tablespoons light corn syrup

1 quart Peaches 'n' Cream Ice Cream (page 34)

Powdered sugar

Caramelized Peaches (recipe follows)

---

1. Freeze the cake until it is firm to the touch, at least 1 hour.

2. Place the cake on a serving plate. Using a long serrated knife, cut a 1-inch-thick layer off the top of the cake and set it aside. Using a small sharp knife, carefully cut around the inside of the cake, leaving a 1-inch shell on the bottom and around the sides. Carefully pull out the center of the cake with your fingers. Cut or tear the cake center into ½-inch pieces and freeze until needed.

3. In a small bowl, mix together the peach brandy, water, and corn syrup. Evenly brush this mixture over the inside of the hollowed-out cake.

4. Soften the ice cream 5 minutes at room temperature or 3 seconds on High in the microwave oven. Transfer to a large bowl. Fold the reserved cake pieces into the ice cream. Fill the cavity of the cake with the ice cream and cake mixture, packing it in tightly to fill air pockets. Replace the top layer of the cake. Cover tightly with plastic wrap and freeze up to 24 hours.

5. To serve, let the cake stand at room temperature 5 to 10 minutes to soften slightly. Dust the top with powdered sugar. Cut into slices with a serrated knife and serve with Caramelized Peaches on the side.

Caramelized Peaches

Makes about 4 cups

---

3 tablespoons unsalted butter
⅓ cup (packed) light brown
  sugar
⅛ teaspoon ground cinnamon

6 firm ripe peaches (about 2 pounds),
  peeled, pitted, and cut into slices ½
  inch thick, or 4 cups frozen unsweetened peach slices, thawed

---

1. In a large heavy skillet, melt the butter over medium heat. Stir in the brown sugar and cinnamon.

2. Add the peaches and cook, stirring gently to coat, until the sauce thickens slightly and the peach slices are just tender, 7 to 9 minutes. Remove from the heat and let cool slightly.

Lemon and Blackberry Ice Cream Cake

This dessert relies on a couple of convenience foods to make a stunning presentation. If you can find a lemon sponge cake, by all means use it. Decorate the top with clusters of blackberries garnished with fresh mint leaves.

Serves 10 to 12

---

1 (10¾-ounce) loaf-shape lemon or plain sponge cake or angel food cake

¼ cup blackberry brandy

1½ quarts Lemon Blackberry Swirl Ice Cream (page 80)

1 (8-ounce) container frozen extra-creamy whipped topping with real cream, thawed

Fresh or frozen unsweetened blackberries and fresh mint leaves, for garnish

---

1. Cut the cake crosswise into ½-inch-thick slices. Arrange the cake slices, overlapping, in the bottom of a lightly oiled 9-inch springform pan. Sprinkle with 2 tablespoons of the blackberry brandy.

2. Soften the ice cream 5 minutes at room temperature or 3 seconds on High in the microwave. Spoon the ice cream evenly over the cake slices, spreading with a spatula and patting down to remove any air pockets.

3. Fold the remaining 2 tablespoons blackberry brandy into the whipped topping and spread over the ice cream. Garnish with the berries. Cover and freeze until firm, at least 6 hours or as long as 3 days.

4. To serve, let thaw 15 minutes at room temperature. Garnish the cake with fresh mint leaves. Run a thin knife around the edges and release the sides of the pan. Cut into wedges with a sharp knife dipped in hot water. Serve on chilled dessert plates.

Frozen Strawberry Shortcake

With this simple recipe, strawberry shortcake can be enjoyed any time of year. Use frozen whipped topping or aerosol whipped cream when you're pressed for time.

Serves 8

---

1 (10¾-ounce) frozen all-butter pound cake

3 tablespoons Chambord, Triple Sec, or orange juice

2 tablespoons strawberry jelly or jam

1 quart Sensational Strawberry Ice Cream (page 28) or strawberry ice cream of choice

1½ cups heavy cream

⅓ cup sifted powdered sugar

Simple Strawberry Sauce (page 187)

---

1. Partially thaw the pound cake, in a microwave if necessary. Cut the cake crosswise into 8 slices. Lay the slices flat on a baking sheet. In a small bowl, whisk 1 tablespoon of the Chambord with the jelly and brush over the cake slices.

2. Soften the ice cream for 5 minutes at room temperature or 3 seconds on High in the microwave. Spoon ½-cup portions of ice cream onto each slice, spreading into an even layer. Place in the freezer while you whip the cream.

3. In a large mixing bowl, combine the cream, powdered sugar, and remaining 2 tablespoons Chambord. Beat with an electric mixer on medium speed until soft peaks form. Working quickly, spoon or pipe mounds of whipped cream over each slice of cake, covering the ice cream completely. Freeze until firm to the touch, about 30 minutes.

4. Wrap in plastic wrap and freeze at least 6 hours or as long as 3 days. To serve, thaw 10 minutes in the refrigerator. Place each cake slice on a chilled dessert plate and top with about ⅓ cup Simple Strawberry Sauce.

Black Bottom Grasshopper Ice Cream Pie

First came the grasshopper cocktail of the 1950s, and then the next decade brought us the popular cream pie. This frozen version eliminates last-minute fuss and adds an extra layer of luscious chocolate. For this recipe, mint lovers may want to make their Chocolate Curls and Twirls from a bar of mint-flavored chocolate.

Serves 8

1½ cups finely ground chocolate wafer cookies (about 30 wafers)

3 tablespoons sugar

5 tablespoons unsalted butter—4 melted and 1 cold, cut into small pieces

½ cup heavy cream

2 ounces bittersweet or semisweet chocolate, finely chopped

5 cups Grasshopper Ice Cream (page 51), Mint Chocolate Chip Ice Cream (page 70), or store-bought mint-flavored ice cream

Chocolate Curls and Twirls (page 93) or finely chopped chocolate, for garnish

---

1. Lightly grease a 9-inch pie plate. In a medium bowl, combine the cookie crumbs and 2 tablespoons of the sugar, tossing to mix. Add the 4 tablespoons melted butter and stir with a fork until the crumbs are moistened. Press into the bottom and up the sides of the prepared pie plate. Freeze until firm, about 30 minutes.

2. In a medium saucepan, combine the cream and the remaining 1 tablespoon sugar. Cook over medium heat, stirring occasionally, until the mixture is slightly thickened and reduced to ⅓ cup, 5 to 7 minutes. Add the 1 tablespoon cold butter and the chocolate and cook, stirring, until melted and smooth.

3. Spread the chocolate cream over the bottom of the crumb crust. Freeze until set, about 1 hour.

4. Soften the ice cream at room temperature for 5 minutes or microwave on High for 3 seconds. Pack into the cold crust, spreading into an even layer over the chocolate. Cover with Chocolate Curls and Twirls. Freeze until firm, at least 6 hours or as long as 3 days. Let stand at room temperature 10 to 15 minutes before slicing with a long sharp knife dipped in hot water. Serve on chilled dessert plates.

Coffee Toffee Ice Cream Mud Pie

There seem to be hundreds of versions of this all-American favorite. This one has plenty of "mud," which appeals to all the middle-aged "kids" in my neighborhood.

Serves 8

---

15 chocolate creme sandwich cookies, such as Oreos

3 tablespoons butter, melted

5 cups Mocha Ice Cream (page 23) or your favorite brand premium coffee ice cream

1 (5-ounce) package chocolate-covered English toffee candy bars (such as Heath Bars), chopped (about ¾ cup)

¾ cup Hot Brandied Fudge Sauce (page 83) or jarred fudge sauce, at room temperature

½ cup chopped salted or unsalted peanuts, or toasted almonds or pecans

---

1. Beat the cookies in half and place them in a food processor or blender. Pulse on and off until the cookies are finely chopped. Add the melted butter and process until well mixed. Press the crumbs into the bottom and sides of a lightly greased 9-inch pie plate. Freeze until firm, about 30 minutes.

2. Soften the ice cream 5 minutes at room temperature or 3 seconds on High in the microwave. Spoon half of the ice cream into the chilled crust, pressing down to remove any air pockets. Top with an even layer of chopped toffee bars. Top with an even layer of the remaining ice cream, pressing down to remove air pockets. Cover and freeze until firm, about 4 hours.

3. Spread an even layer of Hot Brandied Fudge Sauce over the frozen pie and sprinkle with the nuts. Freeze until firm, at least 6 hours or as long as 3 days. Thaw 10 minutes in the refrigerator before serving. Cut into wedges with a sharp knife dipped in hot water.

Frozen Lemon Meringue Pie

Think of this as a latter-day baked Alaska: cool lemon custard ice cream in a crunchy graham cracker crust, topped with a golden cloud of freshly baked meringue. This may be the easiest lemon pie you've ever made.

Serves 8

1½ cups graham cracker crumbs or 1 (5⅓-ounce) package from a 1-pound box of graham crackers, finely ground (about 22 squares)
¾ cup sugar, preferably superfine
¼ teaspoon ground cinnamon (optional)
1 stick (4 ounces) unsalted butter, melted

5 cups Lemon Custard Ice Cream (page 36)
5 egg whites
1 teaspoon vanilla extract
¼ teaspoon cream of tartar
Dash of salt

---

1. In a medium bowl, combine the graham cracker crumbs, ¼ cup of the sugar, and the cinnamon; toss to mix. Add the melted butter, stirring with a fork until the crumbs are evenly moistened. Empty the mixture into a lightly greased 9-inch pie plate, pressing the crumbs evenly all around the bottom and sides of the plate. Freeze until firm, about 30 minutes.

2. Soften the ice cream 5 minutes at room temperature or 3 seconds on High in the microwave. Spread the ice cream evenly in the cold crust, pressing down to remove any air pockets. Freeze until very firm, at least 8 hours or as long as 3 days.

3. When ready to serve, preheat the oven broiler and position the rack 4 to 6 inches from the heat. In a large mixer bowl, beat together the egg whites, vanilla, cream of tartar, and salt until soft peaks form. While still beating, gradually add the remaining ½ cup sugar. Beat until stiff and glossy peaks form.

4. Remove the pie from the freezer. Working quickly, first spread the meringue around the edges of the pie, making sure to seal it well to the crust. Fill in the center with the rest of the meringue, making swirls. Immediately broil just until the meringue peaks turn golden brown, 1 or 2 minutes. Do not let burn. Serve at once. Return any leftovers to the freezer and serve frozen.

Frozen Pumpkin Pie Deluxe

Fussy eaters who might consider pumpkin pie "yukky" rarely pass on a double dose of ice cream in a snappy crust with two rich sauces. This may be that special make-ahead dessert bound to please everyone at your holiday table.

Serves 8 to 10

---

3 cups finely ground gingersnap cookies (about 13½ ounces)

½ cup (packed) light brown sugar

1 teaspoon ground ginger

1½ sticks (6 ounces) unsalted butter, melted

1¾ quarts Pumpkin Ice Cream with Hazelnuts and Chocolate (page 74) or store-bought pumpkin ice cream

¾ cup Bittersweet Fudge Sauce (page 84), at room temperature

2 cups Brown Sugar Ice Cream (page 44) or store-bought caramel or vanilla ice cream

¾ cup Best Butterscotch Sauce (page 90) or jarred butterscotch sauce, at room temperature

---

1. Light grease a 9-inch springform pan. In a large bowl, stir together the gingersnap crumbs, brown sugar, ginger, and melted butter until evenly mixed. Press the crumbs over the bottom and up the sides of the prepared pan. Freeze until firm, about 30 minutes.

2. Soften the pumpkin ice cream 5 minutes at room temperature or 3 seconds on High in the microwave. Pack into the cold crust, spreading into an even layer. Freeze until just set, about 1 hour. Top with a layer of fudge sauce and freeze until firm, at least 2 hours.

3. Soften the Brown Sugar Ice Cream 5 minutes at room temperature or 3 seconds in the microwave. Spread in an even layer over the fudge sauce. Freeze until just set, about 1 hour. Top with an even layer of Best Butterscotch Sauce. Using a skewer or the pointed tip of a small knife, swirl the sauce into the top inch of the ice cream layer to create a marbleized pattern. Freeze until firm, at least 6 hours or as long as 3 days.

---

4. Run a small sharp knife around the sides of the pan to loosen. Release and remove the sides of the springform. Let the pie stand 5 to 10 minutes at room temperature to soften slightly. Cut into wedges with a long sharp knife dipped in hot water.

Fruited Frozen Trifle

A towering trifle layered in a clear glass bowl always draws rave reviews. Go ahead and bask in your glory. Assembling this frozen version in advance makes for a very cool host.

Serves 10 to 12

½ pint fresh raspberries or 1 cup frozen unsweetened raspberries

1 (10¾-ounce) frozen all-butter pound cake, thawed

½ cup Chambord or peach brandy

½ cup plus 1 tablespoon seedless red raspberry jam

2 cups Peaches 'n' Cream Ice Cream (page 34), softened slightly

2 medium peaches (about ¾ pound), peeled, pitted, and sliced, or 1 cup frozen unsweetened peach slices

2 cups Red Raspberry Frozen Yogurt (page 120), softened slightly

½ cup cold heavy cream

¼ cup sifted powdered sugar

1 teaspoon vanilla extract

2 tablespoons toasted sliced almonds

---

1. If using fresh raspberries, rinse gently and drain in a colander. Pick over to remove any badly bruised or moldy fruit.

2. Cut the cake crosswise into slices ½ inch thick. Lay the pieces flat on a clean work surface and brush with the Chambord. Cut each cake slice diagonally into 2 triangles.

3. To assemble the trifle, heat the jam in a microwave or over low heat until melted when stirred. In a 2- or 2½-quart clear glass serving bowl, arrange 8 or 10 cake triangles to cover the bottom of the dish and curve up the sides of the bowl slightly. Brush or spread 3 tablespoons of jam over the cake. Spoon in the peach ice cream, packing down to remove any air pockets. Top with ¾ cup peach slices, reserving the rest for garnish.

4. Top with another 6 or 8 cake triangles and brush or spread with 3 tablespoons jam. Spoon in the raspberry yogurt, packing down to remove air pockets. Top with ¾ cup of the raspberries, the remaining cake slices, and the remaining jam.

5. In a medium mixer bowl, combine the cream, powdered sugar, and vanilla. Beat with an electric mixer on medium speed until soft peaks form. Spoon or pipe the whipped cream on top and garnish with the reserved peaches and raspberries. Sprinkle with the toasted almonds. Freeze, uncovered, until firm to the touch, about 30 minutes. Wrap in plastic wrap and freeze at least 6 hours or as long as 3 days. Before serving, refrigerate 10 to 15 minutes to soften. Use a large spoon to scoop out and serve.

Fudgy Strawberry Charlotte

A bevy of berries get added texture and flavor from rich milk chocolate and hazelnuts. Look for Nutella on the same shelf as peanut butter at many supermarkets or in specialty food stores.

Serves 12 to 14

---

1 tablespoon granulated sugar
1 (5-ounce) package ladyfingers (about 18)
⅓ cup hazelnut liqueur, such as Frangelico, or dark rum
1½ quarts Sensational Strawberry Ice Cream (page 28)
1 (13-ounce) jar creamy chocolate hazelnut spread, such as Nutella

3 cups Strawberry Daiquiri Sorbet (page 154)
½ cup cold heavy cream
¼ cup sifted powdered sugar
Coarsely chopped toasted hazelnuts, for garnish
Simple Strawberry Sauce (recipe follows)

---

1. Lightly oil or butter a 9-inch springform pan. Coat the bottom and sides of the pan with the granulated sugar.
2. Trim about ½ inch off one end of each ladyfinger, reserving the cut pieces. Brush the ladyfingers and the cut pieces on all sides with ¼ cup of the liqueur.
3. Line the sides of the pan with a row of ladyfingers, placing them upright with cut ends down, with the flat sides facing the inside of the pan. Place the remaining ladyfingers and cut pieces in a single layer on the bottom of the pan. Freeze until firm, about 30 minutes.
4. Soften the ice cream for 5 minutes at room temperature or 3 seconds on High in the microwave. Spoon the ice cream into the chilled pan, pressing down to remove any air

pockets. Using a small spoon, drop half of the Nutella by teaspoons over the ice cream, spacing the drops evenly; do not spread. Cover and freeze until firm, about 4 hours.

5. Soften the sorbet 5 minutes at room temperature or 3 seconds on High in the microwave. Spoon the sorbet over the frozen Nutella, spreading in an even layer and pressing down to remove any air pockets. Drop the remaining Nutella by teaspoons over the sorbet, spacing the drops evenly; do not spread. Cover again and freeze for 30 minutes.

6. In a medium mixer bowl, combine the cream, powdered sugar, and remaining 1 tablespoon liqueur. Beat with an electric mixer on medium speed until soft peaks form.

7. Place the springform pan on a serving plate. Run a thin knife along the sides of the pan to free the ladyfingers. Release and remove the sides of the springform. Spoon or pipe the whipped cream on top. Garnish with chopped nuts. Freeze until firm to the touch, about 30 minutes. Wrap in plastic wrap and freeze at least 6 hours or as long as 3 days. Serve with Simple Strawberry Sauce.

Simple Strawberry Sauce

Makes about 3 cups

---

3 (10-ounce) packages frozen sweetened strawberries, thawed

---

1. Puree the berries with their juices in a food processor or blender. Strain to remove the seeds, if desired.

2. If made in advance, cover and refrigerate up to 2 days.

Ice Cream Cassata

Cassata, *a popular Sicilian dessert, can be either a fruit-filled ice cream or a rich layer cake made with ricotta cheese, candied fruits, chocolate, and cream. Of course, it's the frozen version I present here. The convenience of serving this cassata gelata is surpassed only by its luxurious texture and complex flavor, reminiscent of spumoni. When time permits, seek out quality candied fruits from gourmet shops or baking product catalogs.*

Serves 8 to 10

¾ cup mixed candied fruit, chopped
3 tablespoons dark rum or amaretto
2 tablespoons orange liqueur, such as
   Triple Sec
4 ounces bittersweet or semisweet chocolate, well chilled
1 quart pistachio ice cream, homemade
   (page 32) or store-bought

¾ cup cold heavy cream
¾ cup Chocolate Rum Sauce (page 87)
   or jarred chocolate sauce
Maraschino cherries (with stems), for
   garnish

---

1. In a small bowl, gently mix together the candied fruit, rum, and orange liqueur. Cover and refrigerate at least 1 hour to blend the flavors.
2. Using the large holes on a cheese grater, shred the cold chocolate into coarse pieces. Place in a small bowl, cover, and refrigerate until needed.
3. In a large bowl, let the ice cream soften 5 minutes at room temperature or 3 seconds on High in the microwave. Line a 9×5×3-inch loaf pan with plastic wrap, pressing it well into the corners, allowing a 2-inch overhang on each end.

4. In another large bowl, whip the cream to soft peaks. Fold in the fruit-rum mixture and the chocolate pieces. Fold this whipped cream mixture into the softened ice cream until well blended.

5. Pour the ice cream mixture into the plastic-lined loaf pan. Tap the pan against a cutting board several times to fill the corners and remove any air pockets. Cover with plastic wrap and freeze at least 8 hours or as long as 3 days.

6. Remove the plastic wrap and invert the pan on a chilled platter; peel off the remaining plastic wrap. Using a hot knife dipped in hot water, cut into slices ¾ inch thick. Serve on chilled dessert plates. Drizzle each serving with about 1 tablespoon Chocolate Rum Sauce and garnish with a maraschino cherry.

Triple Chocolate Bombe

A layered trio of chocolates is a surefire hit, but don't limit yourself to this one idea. Follow these same instructions to create a classic Neapolitan bombe using chocolate, vanilla, and strawberry, or devise your very own combination of ice creams, frozen yogurts, or sorbets.

Serves 6 to 8

Nonstick cooking spray or flavorless vegetable oil

2 cups Classic Chocolate Ice Cream (page 16) or your favorite brand premium chocolate ice cream, softened slightly

2 cups White Chocolate Ice Cream (page 21) or store-bought ice cream of choice, softened slightly

2 cups Chocolate Malt Ice Cream (page 22), Bittersweet Cocoa Sorbet (page 136), or store-bought chocolate sorbet, softened slightly

1½ cups hot fudge sauce, homemade (page 82) or store-bought

1. Lightly coat the inside of a 6-cup melon-shaped mold (about 9 inches long) with nonstick cooking spray or vegetable oil and freeze until very cold, at least 30 minutes. Alternatively, line a 6-cup bowl with plastic wrap, letting the plastic hang over the sides.
2. Spread an even layer of Classic Chocolate Ice Cream in the bottom and up the sides of the chilled mold. Cover with plastic wrap, pressing against the ice cream to seal it tightly and fill any air pockets. Freeze until very firm, at least 4 hours.
3. Remove the plastic wrap from the mold and pack the White Chocolate Ice Cream into the cavity, pressing down to remove any air pockets; it will only fill the mold partway. Cover with plastic wrap and freeze until firm, at least 4 hours. Repeat with the Chocolate Malt Ice Cream to fill and freeze until very firm, at least 6 hours.

4. Dip the mold into very hot water for 2 seconds. Remove the plastic wrap and invert the mold onto a chilled platter. (If using a bowl, peel off the plastic wrap.) Serve at once or cover and freeze up to 3 days.

5. To serve, cut into ¾-inch-thick slices with a sharp knife dipped in hot water and set on chilled dessert plates. Top each serving with about 3 tablespoons hot fudge sauce, if desired.

Watermelon Bombe

An oval bombe mold is shaped like a watermelon, so why not carry the similarity just a little further? Slice into this ice cream bombe and you'll see pink watermelon, complete with "seeds" and "rind." If you are unable to beg, borrow, or buy a melon-shaped mold, use a 6-cup bowl and make a round watermelon.

Serves 6 to 8

Nonstick cooking spray or 2 teaspoons flavorless vegetable oil

3 cups French Vanilla Ice Cream (page 11) or your favorite brand premium vanilla ice cream, softened slightly

2 tablespoons miniature semisweet chocolate chips

3 cups Watermelon Sorbet (page 152) or store-bought strawberry sorbet, softened slightly (see Note)

Green food coloring

---

1. Lightly coat the inside of a 6-cup melon-shaped mold (about 9 inches long) with nonstick cooking spray or the vegetable oil. Freeze until very cold, at least 30 minutes. Alternatively, line a 6-cup bowl with plastic wrap, letting the plastic hang over the sides; refrigerate until needed.

2. Spread an even layer of vanilla ice cream in the bottom and up the sides of the chilled mold; it will remain hollow in the center. Cover with plastic wrap, pressing against the ice cream to seal tightly and fill any air pockets. Freeze until very firm, at least 4 hours.

3. Fold the chocolate chips into the softened sorbet. Remove the plastic from the mold and pack the sorbet mixture into the cavity, pressing down to remove any air pockets. Cover with plastic wrap and freeze until firm, at least 2 hours.

4. Dip the mold into very hot water for 2 seconds to loosen. Remove the plastic wrap and invert onto a chilled platter. Return to the freezer until the ice cream is firm to the touch, about 15 minutes.

5. Place about 4 drops of green food coloring in a small bowl. Use the undiluted food coloring to paint the outside of the molded ice cream. Do not try for uniform color; variegated stripes are more realistic. Cover with plastic wrap and freeze until very firm, at least 6 hours or as long as 3 days. Cut into ¾-inch-thick slices with a sharp knife dipped in hot water and serve on chilled dessert plates.

NOTE: Because the look is so important here, if the watermelon used for making the sorbet lacks vivid color, you may want to mix 1 drop of red food coloring into the mixture before freezing in the ice cream maker.

Frozen Italian Fantasy

This makes a great finale to an April Fool's dinner . . . any day of the year. Guests will do a double-take when you serve this trompe l'oeil *platter of "spaghetti and meatballs" for dessert, but watch their confusion turn to delight when they find out the "pasta" is ice cream. You'll need a potato ricer for this—a handy gadget that looks like a giant garlic press.*

Serves 4

---

6 to 8 tiny truffles from steps 1 through 3 of Truffled Espresso Bean Ice Cream (page 66)
¼ cup finely chopped toasted walnuts
2 cups French Vanilla Ice Cream (page 11)

½ cup strawberry or raspberry jelly
2 tablespoons chilled, finely grated white chocolate
2 teaspoons finely chopped fresh mint leaves

---

1. Place a 9- or 10-inch serving plate and a potato ricer in the freezer until cold, about 15 minutes.

2. To make the "meatballs," roll the prepared truffles in chopped walnuts to coat. Return to the refrigerator or freezer until needed.

3. Soften the ice cream about 5 minutes at room temperature or microwave on High for 3 seconds. Pack half the ice cream into the chilled potato ricer. Working over the cold serving plate, slowly push the ice cream through the cold ricer, letting the strands of "pasta" fall onto the plate. Repeat with the remaining ice cream. Place the plate in the freezer until the ice cream is firm to the touch, about 15 minutes.

4. To make the "marinara sauce," whisk the jelly in a small bowl until fluid, about 1 minute. Drizzle the jelly over the ice cream "pasta" and sprinkle with the grated white chocolate for "Parmesan cheese." Scatter the nut-coated truffle "meatballs" on top. Sprinkle with mint (to resemble chopped parsley) and serve at once, cutting into individual portions with a large spoon. If made in advance, carefully cover the dessert and freeze up to 3 days. Let soften 5 to 10 minutes in the refrigerator before garnishing with the mint and serving.

Crazy for Coconut Ice Cream Log

Use this same technique to serve any of your favorite cookie and ice cream combos, such as Peppermint Ice Cream (page 50) rolled in chocolate wafer crumbs or Peaches 'n' Cream Ice Cream (page 34) rolled in crumbled amaretti.

Serves 8 to 10

---

3 cups coarsely crumbled Coconut Mocha-Nut Macaroons (20 to 24 cookies; page 76)
1½ quarts Coconut Ice Cream with Chocolate and Roasted Almonds (page 38)
Hot Cocoa Mocha Sauce (page 89) or jarred chocolate sauce

---

1. Spread the macaroon crumbs in an even layer on a baking sheet at least 12 inches long and refrigerate or freeze. Freeze a serving platter at least 10 inches long.
2. Spoon the ice cream onto the center of an 18-inch piece of heavy-duty aluminum foil. Lift the short ends of the foil to meet in the center, loosely covering the ice cream. Using your hands, press against the foil to form the ice cream into a cylinder about 10 inches long. Wrap the sides of the foil tightly around the ice cream, taking care to make the cylinder as compact and smooth as possible. Freeze until hard, about 4 hours.
3. Remove the ice cream cylinder and the pan of chilled macaroon crumbs from the freezer. Unwrap the ice cream log and discard the foil. Working quickly, roll the ice cream cylinder in the crumbs, gently pressing as you roll to coat. Place on a chilled platter, cover, and freeze until firm, at least 6 hours or as long as 3 days.
4. To serve, cut into 1-inch pieces with a sharp knife dipped in hot water. Serve with Hot Cocoa Mocha Sauce.

Chocolate Birds' Nests with Tropical Flavors

These chocolate candy "nests" are pretty rich on their own, so I like to use them for serving a light ice cream or sorbet. If you happen to have an oval-shaped scoop, your ice cream will truly resemble an egg. Look for crisp chow mein noodles in cans or plastic bags in the Asian foods section of most supermarkets.

Serves 4

---

1 cup semisweet chocolate chips
(6 ounces)
1½ tablespoons honey
1¼ cups chow mein noodles (about 2 ounces)
½ cup coarsely chopped salted or unsalted peanuts

2 cups Coconut Ice (page 139), Mango Margarita Sorbet (page 144), or store-bought mango sorbet
1 cup Mango-Ginger Sauce (page 128)
Caramel Icicles (page 96; optional)

---

1. In a 2-quart glass bowl, melt the chocolate chips with the honey in a microwave oven on High for 2 to 2½ minutes, stirring twice. Alternatively, melt in a double boiler, stirring, over low heat.

2 Gently fold the noodles and peanuts into the chocolate mixture to coat. Spoon the chocolate-noodle mixture onto a wax paper-lined baking sheet, making 4 mounds about 3 inches in diameter. Use a large spoon to make a deep indentation in the center of each mound; spread out the sides and mold into a round nest about 4 inches in diameter. Refrigerate the nests until firm, about 30 minutes. If made in advance, cover and refrigerate up to 5 days.

3. Place a large scoop of Coconut Ice in each nest and top with ¼ cup Mango-Ginger Sauce. Stick 1 or 2 Caramel Icicles in each scoop and serve at once.

Berry Sundaes in Chocolate Shells

Large scallop shells from cookware shops are traditionally used for serving Coquilles St. Jacques, *but they are also perfect for making edible chocolate dishes. These require a little time and a bit of patience, but the results are most impressive. If you are serving more than one Valentine, the recipe can easily be doubled or tripled.*

Serves 2

---

2 teaspoons flavorless vegetable oil

8 ounces imported white chocolate, or bittersweet or semisweet chocolate, finely chopped

1½ cups Spiced Raspberry Sorbet (page 151) or store-bought raspberry sorbet

¼ cup Raspberry Puree (page 126), Very Berry Sauce (page 127), or store-bought chocolate syrup

Fresh raspberries, for garnish

---

1. Turn 2 (5-inch) scallop shells upside down and cover the *outside* of the shells first with a layer of plastic wrap and then with a layer of aluminum foil. (The plastic wrap provides added strength and give to the foil, needed later when unmolding.) Wrap the shells snugly, pressing down firmly to pick up the impression of the natural ridges and indentations. Take your time, as this attention to detail determines the final appearance of the chocolate shells. Lightly brush the foil with oil. Place the shells, foil-side up, on a wax paper-lined baking sheet.

2. Carefully melt the chocolate in the top of a double boiler over very low heat, stirring until smooth. Remove from the heat and let the chocolate cool until slightly thickened, 5 to 10 minutes.

3. Spoon all but 2 tablespoons of the melted chocolate equally over the foil-covered shells. Using a narrow metal spatula or a dull knife, spread a thick layer of chocolate evenly and smoothly to within $\frac{1}{16}$ inch of the shells' edges. (Do not let chocolate drip over the edges of shells, though, as it may cause breakage.) Refrigerate until very firm, at least 2 hours.

4. Gently remove the foil and plastic wrap from the shells; the chocolate will still be attached to the foil. Slowly and carefully pull the foil away from the chocolate, using the plastic wrap for leverage and loosening the edges with a knife if necessary. Gently place the chocolate shells, hollow sides up, on the baking sheet. Touch the chocolate as little as possible to avoid fingerprints and smudging. If the chocolate is soft, refrigerate or freeze the shells on the baking sheet until it hardens.

5. Gently reheat the remaining 2 tablespoons chocolate. Using a small brush, patch any cracks or other imperfections with the reserved melted chocolate. Refrigerate or freeze the shells on the baking sheet until the chocolate is set; then cover and refrigerate until needed.

6. Place 2 scoops of sorbet in each of the chocolate shells. Top each with 2 tablespoons Raspberry Puree. Garnish with fresh berries, if desired.

Chocolate Waffles Gone Bananas

Ever since Thomas Jefferson introduced the waffle iron to the United States in the 1700s, inventive cooks have developed hundreds of ways to enjoy this crispy favorite. My friend and fellow cookbook author Marlena Spieler came up with the idea of using prepared cake mix as waffle batter. Serve this extravagant sundae for breakfast if Mom's not looking, or enjoy it anytime as a whimsical dessert. If you're pressed for time or don't own a waffle iron, heat frozen buttermilk waffles in the toaster instead of making your own chocolate ones.

Serves 4

---

1 (1-pound, 2.25-ounce) package devil's food or other chocolate cake mix, or 4 cups prepared homemade chocolate cake batter

3 tablespoons vegetable oil

½ cup maple syrup

3 tablespoons dark rum

2 large, firm ripe bananas

2 cups Maple Walnut Ice Cream (page 29) or Banana Nut Light Ice Cream (page 105)

4 small fresh mint sprigs, for garnish

---

1. Preheat your waffle iron according to the manufacturer's instructions.

2. Prepare the cake mix as the package directs. Brush the waffle grid lightly with oil and ladle the batter into the iron. Bake until the waffles are cooked through and crisp at the edges, about 5 minutes. Remove carefully, as these waffles are very tender (see Note). Repeat with the remaining batter. Keep the waffles warm or let cool and then freeze for future use.

3. In a medium skillet, warm the maple syrup and rum over medium heat. Peel the bananas and cut them diagonally into slices ½ inch thick. Add the banana slices to the syrup mixture and toss gently to coat. Cook until the sauce has thickened slightly and the bananas are heated through, 2 to 3 minutes.

4. Top each warm waffle with a large scoop of ice cream and one-fourth of the warm bananas and sauce. Garnish with a mint sprig and serve at once.

NOTE: This recipe makes 8 (5-inch square) waffles, allowing a large margin for error. Extra waffles can be wrapped airtight and frozen for future use. Reheat frozen waffles on the low setting in your toaster.

Ice Cream Bonbons

As a kid, one of the best parts of going to the local theater was buying a box of frozen bonbons to eat during the movie. Now I can relive that experience in front of my VCR at home, or, better yet, present my guests with a lovely platter of homemade bonbons for dessert. Choose your favorite ice cream or sorbet to give these your signature touch. And if you want to gild the lily a bit, drizzle the finished bonbons with melted white chocolate or sprinkle with candy cake decorations, such as chocolate jimmies or sprinkles.

Makes about 30

---

1 quart Utterly Peanut Butter Ice Cream (page 37) or flavor of choice
1¼ pounds bittersweet or semisweet chocolate, finely chopped
⅓ cup solid vegetable shortening, such as Crisco

---

1. Freeze 2 or 3 baking sheets or plates lined with wax paper or foil until cold, about 15 minutes. Using a small (1-inch) ice cream scoop, a large melon baller, or a tablespoon, scoop small ice cream balls (1 to 1½ inches in diameter) onto the sheets. Working quickly, insert a toothpick into the center of each ice cream ball. As each sheet is filled, place in the freezer before beginning the next one. Freeze until very firm, about 3 hours.
2. In a double boiler over low heat, melt the chocolate and shortening, stirring, until blended and smooth. Remove from the heat and let cool until tepid and slightly thickened but still liquid, 5 to 10 minutes.
3. Remove one sheet of ice cream balls from the freezer. Using the toothpick as a handle, hold an ice cream ball over the pan of melted chocolate. Ladle the melted chocolate over the ice cream ball, turning the ball to coat it completely and letting the excess chocolate run back into the pan.

4. Place the coated bonbon on the baking sheet and gently remove the toothpick. Decorate if desired. Repeat with the remaining bonbons, returning each sheet to the freezer as it is completed. Freeze until firm, about 30 minutes. Then cover and freeze in a single layer until very firm, at least 4 hours or as long as 2 days.

Cinnamon Ice Cream Tostadas

If you're unable to find "snack size" flour tortillas, cut 4- or 5-inch circles from larger ones.

Serves 4

2 tablespoons sugar
½ teaspoon ground cinnamon
4 small (4- to 5-inch) flour tortillas
3 tablespoons unsalted butter, melted
4 teaspoons Spiced Honey-Bourbon Sauce
   (page 124) or plain honey
3 cups Cinnamon Ice Cream (page 41),
   Cinnamon Fudge Ripple Ice Cream
   (page 75), Double Ginger Ice Cream
   (page 43), or store-bought ice cream of
   choice

¾ cup Rich Chocolate Sauce (page 85)
   or jarred chocolate sauce
4 to 8 Caramel Icicles; optional (page 96)

1. Preheat the oven to 350°F. In a small bowl, mix the sugar and cinnamon. Brush both sides of the tortillas with melted butter and arrange in a single layer on a buttered baking sheet. Sprinkle the cinnamon-sugar evenly over 1 side of each tortilla.
2. Bake until the tortillas are crisp and golden brown, 10 to 12 minutes. The cinnamon tortillas can be made in advance and stored at room temperature up to 8 hours. If desired, warm in a 350°F. oven 3 to 5 minutes before serving.
3. Just before serving, place the tortillas on dessert plates and drizzle 1 teaspoon Spiced Honey-Bourbon Sauce over each. Top with 2 medium-size scoops of ice cream and 3 tablespoons chocolate sauce. Garnish with 1 or 2 Caramel Icicles if you like. Serve at once.

Lickety-Split Ice Cream Sandwiches

These sweet little ice cream sandwiches are just the thing to serve as a light dessert on any casual occasion. After a backyard barbecue, just pile the wrapped frozen sandwiches in a napkin-lined basket and pass them to your guests. Depending upon the number being served, you may also want to tuck a small block of frozen gel refrigerant in the basket to keep things cold.

Makes 8

---

16 crisp chocolate wafer cookies
1 cup French Vanilla Ice Cream (page 11) or any other flavor ice cream, sorbet, or frozen yogurt—homemade or store-bought—softened slightly

⅓ cup finely chopped candy, such as Heath Bars, peppermint candies, or candy cake decorations, such as chocolate jimmies or sprinkles, or plain or toasted coconut

---

1. Arrange 8 cookies flat-side up in a baking pan or plate. Using a small (1-inch) ice cream scoop or a spoon, place a heaping tablespoon of ice cream on each. Cover with the remaining cookies, pressing down gently to form a sandwich. Smooth the edges, if desired.

2. Pat the chopped candy onto the ice cream around the edges or roll the sandwiches in candy to coat. Freeze uncovered until firm to the touch, about 30 minutes.

3. Wrap the sandwiches individually in plastic wrap or wax paper and freeze until hard, at least 2 hours or as long as 3 days.

NOTE: Almost any cookie, store-bought or homemade, can be used in this manner. For variation, use oatmeal or chocolate chip cookies, brownies, or madeleines.

Index

Plugged In
The best recipes for your small appliances!

THE BEST BREAD MACHINE COOKBOOK EVER

MADGE ROSENBERG

THE BEST LOW-FAT, NO-SUGAR BREAD MACHINE COOKBOOK EVER

MADGE ROSENBERG

THE BEST BREAD MACHINE COOKBOOK EVER
ETHNIC BREADS

MADGE ROSENBERG

THE BEST FRYER COOKBOOK EVER

PHYLLIS KOHN

THE BEST SLOW-COOKER COOKBOOK EVER

NATALIE HAUGHTON

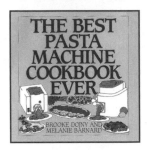

THE BEST PASTA MACHINE COOKBOOK EVER

BROOKE DOJNY AND MELANIE BARNARD

THE BEST PRESSURE COOKER COOKBOOK EVER

PAT DAILEY

THE BEST ICE CREAM MAKER COOKBOOK EVER

PEGGY FALLON

THE BEST STEAMER COOKBOOK EVER

MARGE FOORE